A ROADMAP THROUGH LIFE

Lessons Learned

**If Only I Knew Then
What I Know Now**

Kurth Krause

First Edition

Copywrite © 2020 by Kurth Krause

−All rights reserved−

It is not legal to reproduce, duplicate, or transmit any part of this document in either electronic means or printed format. Recording of this publication is strictly prohibited.

Website: www.kurthkrause.com

golfnspace@aol.com

paperback: ISBN 978-0-9984568-2-9

eBook: ISBN 978-0-99884568-3-6

Reviews of previous book by Kurth Krause:

Amazon Five-Star Reviews for
My 36 Years in Space

"A great read. Kurth Krause, an American hero, refreshingly takes us down memory lane when we as Americans were so proud of our achievements in space exploration."

"The True Space Heroes. A truly mesmerizing read. This book presents our space accomplishments from the point of view of the support staff. You won't be able to put this book down!"

"A Thrilling Ride through Space. Wow! What an exciting read. Mr. Krause takes us on an "edge of the chair ride" through his aerospace career. A fascinating story of a true space pioneer.

"This account will provide an appreciation of this time in our history that is truly unique. If you have any interest in our space program history, this is a worthwhile read."

"Every event and launch brought me back to the events playing out in my own life. This is a great read with beautiful pictures placed at exactly the right places to answer my questions immediately."

"What a great read. Keeps you on edge throughout. Hard to put down. What an amazing ride. I read the book twice."

"An inside view of the Apollo missions and what it took to get there. A great and thrilling ride. Hard to put down."

DEDICATION

I dedicate this book to my readers. Each of you have had to make choices at key points in your lives and will have many more opportunities to do so. This book is designed to give you some help in making those important decisions that will affect your personal relationships, your personal finances, and your life. This help is based on my life experiences, decisions, and choices. Some are based on positive decisions I have made to enable a fulfilling life, but I also offer lessons learned–decisions I wish I had made differently. I offer these to help you, the reader, choose judiciously. Yes, this book gives advice, but does so without judgment or pressure. The book offers it in a non-threating way for you to accept or reject at your leisure.

I specifically dedicate the book to my four grandchildren: Rachel Krause, Karissa Krause, Taylor Odish, and Griffin Gildea in hopes that they may benefit on their roadmap through life.

CONTENTS

1. INTRODUCTION 1
2. RELATIONSHIPS SHOULD BE NURTURED 3
3. HOW IMPORTANT IS EDUCATION? 14
4. FINDING A JOB 20
5. IS MONEY CRITICAL? 26
6. ECONOMICS OF BUYING AND SELLING CARS 29
7. HEALTH IS VITAL 39
8. CHOICE OF HOBBIES CAN ENHANCE LIFE 45
9. AMERICAN POLITICS 70
10. INVESTMENTS– DO IT YOURSELF 73
11. HOUSING CHOICES 91
12. INSURANCE TRADEOFFS 95
13. RETIREMENT FINANCES 98
14. TRAVELING THE WORLD 101
15. RELIGION – NEVER TOO LATE 152
16. HAPPINESS IS A CHOICE 158
BIBLIOGRAPHY 162
ACKNOWLEDGEMENTS 164
ABOUT THE AUTHOR 165

1. INTRODUCTION

As each of us charts our course through life, we make numerous important choices that have profound effects on our happiness, health, and prosperity. I am no exception. I often wished there were a good book out there that could have helped me with these difficult choices, educating me on the pros and cons, thus minimizing the mistakes I have made and reinforcing good choices.

I concluded the best way to provide these life experiences and choices was to document them in a book that might be read by my descendants. They could accept or reject the underlying advice in a non-threatening way, at their leisure and at their own pace. I do not mean to imply by the title that these are the only choices in life that are important. Rather these are choices in which I believe my experiences have something to offer.

Perhaps most of us tend to reject unsolicited advice. Maybe that is why we hear that experience is the best teacher. I know I tend to learn from my own mistakes. According to Henry Ford, "The only real mistake is the one from which we learn nothing." I offer this book primarily to those people in their early adulthood where key decisions are beginning to be made. But even in our advanced years we make important decisions which can benefit from sound advice and my own lessons learned along the way.

As I traveled through life, I made my decisions which affected my journey profoundly. Some decisions were good, others not. I often wished I had a wise bird on my shoulder to whisper in my ear to warn me about the bad decisions. I suppose we all wish we had such a wise bird.

Yes, I could have listened to my parents. They certainly had my best interests at heart. But do we listen to our parents? To paraphrase an old saying: as a child I listened, but as a teen I knew better; it was not until later in life that I was surprised at how smart my parents had become. True, they did not graduate from high school and had quit school to work during the depression. But at least I learned by their example to work hard, save money, enjoy life, and become financially self-sufficient.

This is my attempt to be that wise bird for you, my readers. My aspiration is to provide good, perhaps great advice for you, your children, and your grandchildren. Most important is that this advice is in written form for you to accept or reject without judgment from anybody. Verbally offering advice to anyone can be threatening and not taken with an open mind. I know. What gives me the right to offer it? My 79 years of life experience. No, it is probably not infallible, but is intended to help live lives.

So, sit back, read, and accept or reject the advice in the confines of your room without risk. Please let me know if it has been of value to you.

2. RELATIONSHIPS SHOULD BE NURTURED

This may be the most important topic which hopefully lasts one's entire lifetime. Relationships meant something valuable as I was growing up. Now, at age 79, they have even more meaning to me.

Friends

During my childhood, I learned the importance of having one or two good friends. My social needs only developed further as I grew older. Now, I try to make friends every chance I get. I regret I did not maintain the relationships I had during my youth. I would love to reconnect with friends made during my formative years as well as with my college fraternity brothers. At the times I moved to another state, I just let them be reduced to Christmas cards at most and poured myself into my career and family. In the past 20-30 years I have done a better job maintaining these friendships, even distant ones. Of course, having the means to travel and the use of emails make this easier.

Today we live in a villa in a new Continuing Care Residential Community (CCRC) in Southern California with more than 350 people. We all have dinner in the clubhouse, which gives us many opportunities to make new friends our age. Although we have been here only one year, we have had dinner with more than half the residents and are pleased at how social almost everyone is. Most are retired professionals. My wife, Sue, and I make it a point to meet these people and make new friends. This has enriched our lives here. This is an attitude I wish I had developed earlier in life.

Choosing a Life Partner

Although I was in no hurry, I seriously began looking for a prospective wife my junior year in college. Up to that time I just enjoyed dating many girls, but not in the context of marrying. I met Sue, the love of my life, on the University of Wisconsin student train to California for the 1960 Rose Bowl. At the time I was dating two girls in my hometown of Milwaukee and one on the Madison campus. Sue and I began dating immediately. We had much in common: same age, same year in college, career aspirations, loved golf, enjoyed ballroom dancing, had a mutual attraction, and close family ties. And she pretended to like my singing. I learned that dating more than one girl benefited me, as a little jealousy helped. But when Sue gave me an ultimatum, I stopped dating the other girls.

Nevertheless, we do have our differences: Sue is a right-brained artist and Registered Occupational Therapist, while I am a left-brained astronautical engineer and author. Therefore, we complement each other's thinking on important decisions. We have an equal partnership. But we also respect each other's independence. We obviously chose well, as we have been happily married for 57 years.

I recently read a best-seller book, *Men Are from Mars, Women Are from Venus*, which has some valuable advice on how to deal with our differences. It provides understanding on how to sustain a long, happy marriage. But the book is tedious to read because of its abundance of redundancy. Nevertheless, it is worthwhile to find the imbedded valuable nuggets.

Children

When we first married, we had a difference of opinion on how many children we wanted: I wanted four, Sue two. We did agree to wait at least one year. Two years later, Scott was born. Now I wanted three children; Sue still wanted two. After Sheryl was born, we compromised at two. I am so proud of our children. Sue left her career as an occupational therapist to become a stay-at-home mom. She raised them well. We taught our children to be self-reliant. We did pay for Sheryl's college education (Scott's was paid by the government.) and gave them their first used cars. But after they left the nest, we did not help financially. They indeed have demonstrated their all-important self-reliance.

They have given me so much pleasure at every stage of their lives. I was so proud of Scott when he accepted his appointment to the US Air Force Academy. He retired as a Lieutenant Colonel after 20 years as a pilot. Then he became a Chief of Staff at Homeland Security under President Bush, and after six years in a management role in the private sector, joined President Trump's Transition Team. I was equally proud of

Sheryl's dedication to her education, earning the difficult required grades at a great college to become a bilingual teacher in an elementary school. They are great kids, accomplished adults, and wonderful parents. And now we have been enjoying our special grandchildren over the past three decades. It has been said that grandchildren are your reward for not killing your kids. That does not apply to us. Our four grandchildren have certainly been a blessing, but so have our children.

Carlos

Sue and I volunteered to be mentors to some underprivileged teens through the YMCA program. Sue became a big influence in the lives of her two Hispanic girls. After twenty-five years, she remains in contact. My experience was not as fulfilling.

I volunteered to be a mentor to a high school freshman, Carlos, for the duration of his school years. He spoke perfect English and was a good student who studied every day including weekends. His two sisters also were conversant in English, although their mother spoke mostly Spanish. She was immensely proud of her son's As and Bs. She was grateful for my help with Carlos, whom I saw for a few hours every week for three years. His high school teachers and advisors assured both Carlos and his mother that he could get a full scholarship to almost any college he chose, as the family income was extremely low, and they were living on public assistance. His mother cleaned houses, but his father was no longer in his life, which is why the YMCA asked me to mentor him. Although he had been in the United States since age two, he lacked US citizenship. I researched the program that

Bill Gates had created with one billion dollars set aside for Hispanic student scholarships, but I learned that to qualify, one had to be a US citizen. I marched into the high school to admonish them for filling his head with dreams he could not fulfill. (They had never questioned his citizenship.) I informed Carlos and his mother of the bad news and suggested he apply to the local community college. In his senior year, he broke off our relationship. I have not seen him since but learned he did attend the community college as I suggested.

Gus

I volunteered to support a Christian program called Adult and Teen Challenge. It is nationally recognized to enable young adults to rehabilitate from drug and alcohol addiction and get their lives back together. They boast a 78% success rate (compared to Alcoholics Anonymous' 13% success). The program is intense with 24/7 immersion for at least one year in a Christian-oriented addiction recovery center. To be accepted, they must demonstrate a desire to get clean. Most have hit rock bottom. After twelve months living in a facility to educate, train, and rehabilitate with emphasis on the body, mind, and Bible-based spirit, they are mentored by volunteers before reentering the real world.

They asked me to mentor Gus, a likeable 36-year-old Hispanic man and a US citizen. His mother and father were divorced, but he maintained a good relationship with both. He had held a good job until succumbing to both drugs and alcohol. After losing his job, he cashed in his 401(k) and spent it, triggering a big IRS tax penalty. His faith in Christ had been restored at the center, but we had a long way to go to get him back into society. We developed an excellent relationship with mutual respect. He welcomed my help, in part because my space career impressed him.

First, we had to find employment. I worked with him to create a resume by first listing all his accomplishments and skills. He was fluent in English and Spanish. His problems with police were minimal. I took him to the public library to apply for a card and check out two books on job search. We convinced an Adult and Teen Challenge colleague at my church to hire Gus as a driver for his hotel guests. But when he found out that Gus had lost his driver's license due to a DUI, Gus lost this opportunity. His cousin offered him an intern position at his barber shop, but I convinced him to turn it down because it offered no benefits nor future growth. He successfully applied for a position at Trader Joe's and ultimately thrived there.

Next, we had to rectify his financial obligations. In addition to the IRS fines and interest, he owed his sister and mother money he had borrowed. We prioritized these debts, the tax problems being first. I failed to persuade the IRS agent to reduce his debt, so he paid it off on a schedule to avoid garnisheeing his wages, which would have been a negative for his employment. He repaid the loan to his sister, but his mother refused to take any money from him and cancelled the loan. He finally had achieved freedom from debt.

Gus needed a new car. His jeep would not last much longer. I suggested how to negotiate for a car, then showed him my technique. I was in the market for a new Lexus LS 460. So, I took him with me while I negotiated with two Lexus dealerships, pitting one offer against the other. He learned well from this process. He did not realize that it was a game that could be resolved in favor of the customer.

I worked on generating his past due federal and state income tax returns with Gus looking over my shoulder as a learning experience. I hoped to teach him how, but he was so uncomfortable with the process that I doubt if he did it himself in the future.

Gus asked me to help his younger brother get a job. He is a good-looking young man, speaks English well, and, like Gus, has a personable, but shy demeanor. But when he came to my home to craft his resume, I realized I could not help him. He had been in jail, had been on drugs seven different times, and had too many gaps in his employment record. I still feel bad that I could not help.

The last time I saw Gus, he was doing well. He received a promotion to leadership at Trader Joe's, had moved south, and was dating a young lady. His transformation made me feel great.

My Dad – An Obituary

July 2, 2004

I am writing this story about my dad as Sue and I are preparing to fly to Milwaukee to visit him for perhaps the last time. He is in the hospital, weak and shutting down. I could not sleep last night, thinking about him.

He was born Eugene Ralph Krause, March 22, 1918, in Milwaukee, the oldest of two children. He lived in Wisconsin his entire life. Often mistreated by his parents, he had a rather difficult childhood, which may account for some of his "warts," such as a quick temper. But he was a devoted husband and a hard worker. He quit high school his junior year to get a job during the depression., He married his high school sweetheart, Dorothy Raffel, in 1938. I was born two years later, the oldest of four. (One additional child died at birth due to Rh blood incompatibility.) He held two jobs in the early 1940's, while Mom kept house and began raising a family.

One of my first memories of my relationship with my dad was traumatic, but a good learning experience. I had just turned four years old when I threatened to run away from home one time too many. Dad packed my small suitcase, and, as Mom cried, he showed me to the door. When I got to the corner, I stopped. It was my turn to cry—partly because I missed my parents, partly because I was not allowed to cross the street by myself.

Later that year (1944), we moved into our first home in West Allis, a suburb of Milwaukee on the southwest side. Dad took pride in that large, old, two-story house, which he bought for $8,000 and sold five years later for $16,000. I remember several parties they held at the house, while my sister, Karen, and I tried to sleep upstairs. Whenever the relatives got together, the men would play an obscure card game popular only in Wisconsin (Sheepshead) and Germany (Schafkopf), which required a good blend of skill and luck. I would sit next to my dad and entertain the group by counting his chips, since this invited bad luck. He enjoyed cigars in those days and smoked as many as 14 per day, when he quit cold turkey.

In 1947, Dad was proud to be the first on our block with a television set, a 11.5-inch, round-screen Helicrafter. He enjoyed inviting the neighbors in to watch Milton Berle's hit show, the *Texaco Star Theater*. Prior to TV, his favorite radio show was Jack Webb's *Dragnet*. The four of us would sit around the radio each week to hear it. Dad loved guns and duck hunting with his favorite bird dog, Patty, a springer spaniel, who loved it as much as he did. When she died at age ten, he mourned for months. He had almost every breed of dog since, but none compared with Patty. I loved our family vacations by car to central Wisconsin, and, in 1947, to Canada to visit friends.

Despite his limited formal education, Dad emphasized school, at least for Karen and me. He was immensely proud of my academic and business accomplishments and would brag about his kids every chance he got. He was particularly proud of our son Scott's Air Force Academy appointment and Air Force pilot career. He delighted in witnessing Scott receiving Distinguished Graduate honors from the Secretary of the Air Force. It is remarkable how much alike the three of us looked at the same age.

Dad had to quit his job for health reasons at Plankinton Packing Company in Milwaukee and took a job in sales with the Quality Biscuit Company. Later, he earned a promotion to district sales manager in Eau Claire, Wisconsin in 1949, necessitating our move. There, the police department appointed him honorary deputy sheriff; he spent recreation time at their shooting range. My brother, Kirby, was born in 1951 in Eau Claire. My parents often reminded me of my naiveté at the time, when, upon learning Mom was pregnant, I remarked, "Aren't you a little old to be doing that stuff?"

We returned to the southwest side of Milwaukee in 1951, as Dad was promoted to sales manager. There I had fond memories of playing "catch" with him in the alley behind our house. Neither of us was particularly good at it, because I remember chasing the scuffed baseball down the concrete alley to retrieve it. Kim, my youngest sister, was born in 1955. We moved to New Berlin, Wisconsin just outside Milwaukee County a few months before I went off to college in 1958. They lived there until last month, when Mom sold the house as Dad lay in the hospital.

New management squeezed Dad out of his job with the cookie company. He held several other jobs in sales before retiring with no pension at age 63 and tried to live on minimal savings and

Social Security. In 2001, they ran out of savings, Dad explaining, "I didn't think we'd live this long."

Just before finishing this piece, I called Mom to see how Dad was doing and learned he had died just an hour earlier. I am sorry I did not get to see him in time. The last time we hugged was one year ago.

When my family moved to Texas, we promised to return to Milwaukee at least once each year to visit. We have kept that promise for the past 38 years and will continue to do so while my mother is alive. Kirby now lives in Florida, and Karen in Minnesota. Only Kim remains in Milwaukee; she has been the primary caregiver during these difficult times.

Dad was a devoted and faithful husband for all the 65 years of their marriage. He was proud of each of his children and loved us all dearly. We will miss you, Dad. May the Lord watch over you.

Shelter in Place

As I am writing this book, we are under government orders to be sheltered in place, encouraged not to leave our homes without face masks, and to maintain social distancing at least six feet. To ward off the coronavirus from infecting our community, Reata Glen will not allow any nonresident to enter our gates except the staff and medical personnel. Thus far, this is working as we have had zero cases of COVID-19 infection. But it is taking its toll and causing us to appreciate relationships with humanity. We have not visited our families in more than three months, except virtually via Zoom. We are not supposed to congregate in an assembly, but our need is trumping these guidelines. We are getting together with our neighbors in our back yards, but only with one couple at a time. Perhaps this ordeal will reinforce our appreciation of relationships.

Be forewarned that giving unsolicited advice can hurt a relationship. That well-intended advice can be construed as criticism or judgment and backfire. I know. It has happened to me and almost destroyed a relationship. In part that is why I wrote this book, so you, the reader, can accept or reject the advice without feeling threatened.

3. HOW IMPORTANT IS EDUCATION?

Experts across the world continue to emphasize that education is paramount for successful lives. And it is. But I have learned that, based on my own experience, sometimes the wrong education is not productive.

Learning

To me, learning is much more than education. A good education facilitates learning, but I found I had to embrace the topics delivered in and out of the classroom before I truly learned. I also found I had to enjoy the topic to be motivated to learn. Self-motivation is best, but good teachers can instill and enhance that motivation. We are never too old to learn. Learning keeps us happy. Henry Ford said, "Anyone who stops learning is old, whether at twenty or eighty. Anyone who keeps learning stays young."

Elementary School

In my early years, I was an above average student, but I lacked any special motivation. I believe that had it not been for two key factors, I would not have put education so high in my life priorities and would have continued to get by with just an above average education. One factor was my third-grade teacher. She was the first to show a special interest in me. My prior teachers were not as competent, and it showed. I learned the material but was not really motivated. I did not realize until third grade that I could learn so much from a great teacher. I did not know these teachers existed. She made it fun to learn, and her positive reinforcement made all the difference.

My father was the other key factor which had a big influence on my motivation to learn. At first, he used money as the tool to direct my education path. He gave me one dollar for an *A* and fifty cents for a *B* on my semester report card. But in third grade, when I brought home seven *A*'s and one *B*, he could not afford to pay me. Nevertheless, I got the message that my academic accomplishments made him proud. That never left me and continued to motivate me to achieve through most of my academic career. I always sought his approval, which was a big part of my motivation. But eventually that would change.

High School

I continued to recognize the differences in the quality of my teachers, but my motivation remained strong throughout high school. Maybe the bird on my shoulder kept reminding me how much I enjoyed the plaudits from my parents, relatives, and their friends. I did not let the downers from poor teachers weaken my motivation, but it was a challenge to overcome. In sixth grade for example, the boredom of learning the imports and exports of various countries, or in 11th grade learning the simple, mundane concept of vectors in physics class demonstrated teacher ineptitude. My freshman year in high school exposed a great contrast between my two Spanish teachers. Our first semester we learned so well that the class conversed with each other in Spanish without translating to English in our heads. In the second semester all we learned from the head of the department was how to sing in Spanish–not fun. It is a shame that the strong teacher's union continues to protect the bad teachers through their tenure system, rather than acknowledging and rewarding the great ones. Everyone knows which are capable and which are poor. I had great teachers in math, chemistry, and English. My history teacher terrified me. Although I worked harder in his class than any other, I received the only Bs on my record, keeping me from becoming the class valedictorian.

Career counseling in high school was inadequate. First, I took aptitude tests, which I found worthless. The conclusion that I should pursue a career in accounting proved its folly. I doubted I would ever be happy doing accounting my entire life. But I also received uninformed advice from the "career counselor." Based on my perfect grades in math and science, he said I only had two choices: engineering or teaching. Since I did not want to be a teacher, I enrolled at the University of Wisconsin as a mechanical engineering major. I was bored with my only ME class, and after one semester, had to jump through hoops to convince the Dean of Engineering to allow me to transfer to Letters and Science, enabling me to pursue my real career interest in the US space program with a double major in math and physics. The high school counselor did not realize that this new field, launched by Sputnik, was hungry for graduates in my new majors.

College

My motivation increased another level when I started college. Fear of failure had much to do with it. I realized I would now be competing with the best students in the state. Moreover, at our freshman lecture class, the speaker told us to look to our left and right; only one of the three of us would return for our sophomore year. So, I worked extremely hard and achieved a 3.6 GPA out of 4.0, thanks again to a great teacher's aide in calculus. I had a tough time with it the first six weeks, until he gave me special help outside of class. As a result, I earned a grade of 97 on the final exam and earned an *A* in the course. Moreover, I had such a command of calculus that I earned easy *A*'s each of the next two semesters. Good thing my bird told me to go for extra help. My motivation and desire to learn carried me through my junior year. My excellent professors and challenging physics classes reinforced this motivation. But it did not last.

The classes remained challenging, but my desire was taking lower priority to the fun things in college. Meeting the love of my life replaced my casual dating. As fraternity president I let my administrative duties take precedence over learning. And I learned how to play bridge. I let my high GPA enable me to coast, studying much less. My professors and the material in my advanced classes were no longer as interesting to me. I received the first three *C*'s in my life, lost my scholarship, and fell into depression. If only the bird on my shoulder had told me to take a year off, I might have regained my desire to learn. Instead I went right on to graduate school in physics, intending to get a master's degree. Graduate school clearly became a waste of time with my poor attitude. Only space science interested me, and it was the only course I aced. I did not complete my Master of Science degree and could not wait for the year to end so I could marry Sue and begin my career.

While working, I took some graduate courses at night in quantum mechanics in hopes of accumulating enough credits to complete my MS requirements. But even the interesting, but impractical field of quantum mechanics did not motivate me to really learn, although I did receive A's. It was not until I attended the Massachusetts Institute of Technology that my desire to learn returned. Again, my bird should have told me to change my major to astronautical engineering and transfer to MIT, Cal Tech, or Stanford. My graduate school course work at MIT completely turned me around.

My Advice

Perhaps I can offer a broader lesson learned from all of this. Find one or two subjects you are passionate about, then take courses related to those fields. And they do not have to be college courses leading to a degree. One exception lies in the physical sciences, such as the medical field, engineering, computer science, and technology. A degree in the sciences enables one to learn from the baseline introduced by those who preceded us, avoiding the necessity to "reinvent the wheel." We can stand on the shoulders of these learned pioneers. Also, a college degree shows evidence of intellect, achievement, and self-motivation. Absence of a degree can induce a negative bias.

In the first four years of my career, most of my colleagues had advanced degrees, many had doctorates. Later, as I progressed in management, some of my subordinates had advanced degrees. But, with a few notable exceptions, their performance did not significantly differ from those with a bachelor's degree. I wondered whether the time, effort, and investment for advanced degrees was worth it.

If it is a trade that floats your boat, study how to excel in that trade. Do not waste your time and money learning about a field in which you have no interest. I do not mean that you can slight the three *R*'s; they are fundamental in any walk of life. You should master the English language and grammar. (I cringe every time I hear someone from the media butcher grammar, often misusing the object of a preposition.) But passion in your work means everything. To quote Henry Ford, "The whole secret to a successful life is to find out what is one's destiny to do, and then do it." Make sure it involves work that will be of value to society over the long haul. You must avoid a profession or trade that will eventually be obsolete. Several traditional trades have been overcome by new technologies, particularly by computer software. Your passion can be satisfied in a hobby, but how much richer if it involves your daily work!

4. FINDING A JOB

Depending upon one's career choice, experience, track record, salary level, and the supply/demand environment, finding the right job can be challenging. I recommend reading at least one book on this subject. For a corporate executive job, I found *What Color Is Your Parachute?* and *Rites of Passage at $100,000+* to be helpful. There are many other good books for job search for lower and entry level positions.

The Resume

Although all advice on this subject emphasizes a good resume, I learned it is necessary, but ultimately has little impact on the final job offer. The real objective is to obtain an interview. To this goal, the resume is important because it may be the only thing to introduce your qualifications to acquire the interview. To that extent the resume must be perfect. An imperfect resume will likely eliminate you from consideration. Most hiring supervisors dislike reading numerous resumes to decide whom to invite. Therefore, the resume must be short, eye-catching, and distinct from the other dozens applying for the same job. Yet there is a standard format defined in any book on this subject. The first thing the reader looks for is the job objective. This can be a challenge. If the objective is too general, it can be off-putting. If it is too specific, it may not fit the job opening. The best job objective should be specifically tailored to the job opening. Therefore, a tailored resume is necessary for each job.

Before beginning, make a list of every accomplishment you have performed. From this list you can select a subset to create a resume that attracts the attention of the hiring supervisor if those accomplishments meet his/her needs. If possible, your resume should not show gaps in your employment history nor show you are currently unemployed. These are red flags. Therefore, it is advisable to continuously be aware of other job opportunities while you are employed, just in case. It is always easier to get a new job while currently employed.

Interview Preparation

It bears repeating that securing an interview is the real objective of a job search. Do not go to the interview until you are thoroughly prepared. Learn as much as possible about the position, the company, its products, and services, and prepare a list of important questions that demonstrate your knowledge of the position and the company. I made the terrible mistake of not doing my homework when a top-rated executive recruiter invited me for an interview for a position of vice president. That recruiter never contacted me again.

Dress for the interview consistent with the position. Err on overdressing, rather than dressing down. Be well groomed. This shows respect for the interviewer and the organization. Thank him/her for the interview. Be honest. This is the time to admit you are unemployed, but only if asked about your current employment.

Do not say anything negative about your past or current employers and your supervisors. The interviewer will infer that you may disparage the prospective supervisor someday. I made this mistake at a lunch interview with the CEO of a private company for a vice president role. Even though the interview went very well, I never heard from him again. I am sure that my negative comments about my current employer killed the opportunity. Always deliver a confident, competent, positive attitude without arrogance. Send the interviewer a short letter, thanking him/her for the interview and reinforcing the key points on your qualifications.

Networking

By far, the best way to secure a new job is to utilize the network of colleagues you have developed over the years. It is important to establish these relationships to mutual value and respect while working. Let your contacts know in confidence you are looking and ask if they can suggest a contact. This relieves the pressure on them to tell you they do not have an opening. They may suggest someone who, in turn, suggests another. When my CEO laid me off from my general manager position, I exhausted my network of over fifty colleagues before contacting a retired president whom I had only met twice and did not know well. This was the middle of the 1993 aerospace recession. Ultimately, this led to an important position for me, bypassing their hired executive recruiter who had unsuccessfully interviewed over 100 people for this job.

Negotiating

Once you believe you will get an offer, do not be afraid to ask for a good salary and other concessions. When I interviewed with TRW in 1967, the human resources manager asked what salary I expected. My annual salary at the time was $12,000, but I also had a temporary annual housing allowance of $3,000. So, I asked for $15,000 and that became the offer. In retrospect I could have obtained more. Decades later when unemployed, after five successful interviews with management at the prospective employer, I met with the human resources director and knew that I would get an offer. I asked for a higher salary than they were prepared to pay. When their offer was lower than my request, I asked for a sign-on bonus of $25,000 and got it. In addition, I negotiated 13 weeks' severance pay if they had to lay me off in the recession. Earlier in my career, I did not realize that such a negotiation was possible, especially when I currently did not have a job.

When Joe Saponaro hired me to eventually become the general manager of the Aerospace Systems Group of Intermetrics, I did not ask for a raise, because I had received a substantial raise two weeks earlier from my previous employer and did not think it appropriate to get raises back-to-back. In retrospect, I am sure I could have received another good raise had I asked for it. The lesson is to ask for what you think you are worth and not be intimidated by perceived norms.

Keeping the Job

Obviously, you must work hard and perform well to be successful in your new job. A big part of this is aligning your goals with those of your supervisor and his supervisor. If you disagree with any of these goals, express your disagreement constructively. If your suggestion is not accepted, drop it, and perform your role consistent with management's desires. Similarly persuade your subordinates to accept your goals to perform as a team. Do not let any hidden agenda, particularly your personal dislike of management's style, distract from this path. Everyone should be recognized as a team player, suppressing personal desires in favor of the organization.

Seeking Wealth?

To acquire real wealth, financial security and prepare for a comfortable retirement in one's corporate career, it is necessary to attain upper management in something other than a small business. Bonuses and stock options are important supplements to a large salary. Of course, it is difficult to obtain and retain these sought-after positions. Competition can be fierce.

Another way to acquire wealth is to be the founder of one's own business. But this may be even harder to be successful. More than half start-up business fail, and most owners who succeed are not millionaires. Less than 4% have an annual adjusted gross income of $1,000,000, but 21 % of successful entrepreneurs make over $200,000 per year. The most common reason for failure is not that they do not produce a good product or service, but rather have insufficient capital to survive. They run out of money. Estimating cash flow needs is not easy. For this reason, it is difficult to obtain financing at a reasonable interest rate. Management shortfalls and lack of marketing process are two other contributions to business failures. Few businesses are profitable during their first two years, but no business can survive without profits.

Start-ups are not the only failures. A friend inherited enough cash to buy a small business, thinking this a more likely way to become wealthy than his current role as a mechanical engineer employed by a large company. Although the company offered for sale was not currently making a profit, he decided with enough effort, intelligence, and capital, he could make it a success. After extensive due diligence, he bought it, then studied and worked every facet of the business. He put together a business plan but had no exit strategy. He so believed in his plan that when he ran out of cash, he took out first and second mortgages on his house. Then he secured a loan, putting up his country club membership as collateral, thinking the cash could buy him enough time to turn it around. After nine years, he lost the business and country club membership to creditors. At age 64, he became an insurance salesman and had to work 25 more years to have enough to retire. I suppose the lesson here is when you are in a hole, stop digging.

5. IS MONEY CRITICAL?

    I grew up in a home where money was important because it was scarce. We always had a roof over our heads, food on the table, and adequate clothing for our family of six. We even were able to take short vacations within driving distance of our Wisconsin home, but could not afford any luxuries. We had one secondhand car, could not afford college for me or my younger siblings, and virtually no savings for emergencies and retirement. I had scholarships and summer jobs, allowing me to attend the University of Wisconsin. This background instilled in me strong fiscal conservatism both in my personal life and my political views. I could not understand why anyone would not aspire to be financially self-sufficient.

    Before we got married, I used my personal savings from summer jobs to pay cash for a new Volkswagen Beatle and furnish our tiny apartment. With both of us employed in well-paying jobs, we immediately started saving to buy a home. We made a pact to always pay cash for everything except a home. We would not buy anything else on time to avoid the interest and ensure we could always afford our purchases. We also decided to keep our car as long as reasonable to avoid the large expense of a new car. (We kept this VW for 14 years before selling it.)

This strategy worked great; we never had any debt except for the home mortgage. We avoided paying interest like the plague. I cannot emphasize enough the importance of paying off all bills, especially credit cards on time to avoid the exorbitant interest charges and late fees. We never paid any fees for credit cards. If a card is offered with no fees for the first year, threaten to discontinue the card when the offeror tries to bill you the second year. Usually they will waive the annual fee. You can obtain a card that pays you for using it. My Fidelity VISA card pays me an automatic 2% cash back on all my charges every month.

In 18 months, before Sue quit her job as an occupational therapist to get ready for our expectant first baby, we had saved enough to buy a new model home at a low 5¼ % mortgage. We paid all our bills on time and ended up with an extremely high Fair Isaac Company (FICO) credit rating. The FICO score is an important factor in securing a low interest loan. A good way to ensure on-time payments is to set up automatic payments, provided you monitor the monthly statements to rectify any errors.

I advise not to buy a time-share deal. They may sound wise from the sales pitch, but today many time-share owners are paying a fee to get out of their contract. Generally, they are not a good deal. As much as 50% of your initial payment goes to the smooth-talking salesman's commission and to pay for the "free gift" you received for attending the sales pitch. The biggest problem is you must pay for annual maintenance of the property, which can average $2000 per year, with no limit on yearly increases, for the rest of your life. However, I do know a few people who derived benefit from time-shares. They use it every year and intend to continue doing so for the foreseeable future.

I told Sue we would never be rich (she came from upper middle class, as her father had his own small business), but I believed we could live comfortably on my engineer's salary as long as my skills were in demand and we adhered to our strategy. This served us well. It helped that I advanced to middle management by age 34, my salary increasing faster than I had planned. We had saved and invested enough that we joined a country club, traveled the world extensively, retired at age 58, and ended up with two luxury cars. Without this fiscally conservative strategy, this would not have been possible. Had the wise bird been on my shoulder, it might have been pleased.

Is money critical? It certainly can be if the bills are piling up with no good solution, or if you run out of money while in retirement. I do believe the adage that money cannot bring happiness, but lack of it can bring misery. Of course, investing wisely can be critical. It is in this realm that I could have used the wise bird's whisperings.

6. ECONOMICS OF BUYING AND SELLING CARS

Buying and selling cars has always been a difficult and challenging process if one intends on minimizing what you must shell out for a new car and maximizing the price you get for your old one. No purchase except a house can impact your net worth more than an automobile due to depreciation. If you buy a new car every three years, it could cost you more than $500,000 over your lifetime and much more if you buy luxury cars. Therefore, in this chapter I will share what I have learned through my experiences in hopes it will help others financially. Of course, there are criteria other than economics for buying a new car. But too often, in my opinion, emotional forces dominate, causing us to make decisions we later regret when we fully realize their monetary impact. Car salesmen depend on these emotional forces. Almost all of us love to upgrade to a new car. The trick is to balance these desires with their cost. Safety is, of course, important and should be considered in making decisions, but these needs can be satisfied without letting emotions trigger a decision that ignores the financial tradeoffs.

How long should I keep a car?

I learned at an early age that buying a new car too often is a costly way to satisfy transportation needs. My paternal grandfather bought a new, full-size GM car every two-three years until he died at age 89. Yet I doubt he drove more than 1,000 miles per year since his medical retirement at age 50. The value of his estate when he died was small. I am sure that depreciation, insurance, and trading his previous cars with the dealer cost him dearly. My father followed a similar pattern with used cars until he realized that he could no longer afford this practice. He realized it too late. Economics forced him to keep his last car more than twelve years. He ran out of money a few years before he died.

I unexpectedly bought my first new car as an adult after graduate school. I had lent my fiancée my six-year old Volkswagen Beetle, which I had purchased used, a few years earlier. Unfortunately, while she was driving it on the highway, it suddenly stopped. Both the engine and transmission were ruined; the necessary repairs were more than the car was worth. My summer jobs and my scholarships had enabled me to save a good nest egg for our upcoming marriage and start in adult life. My father negotiated with the VW dealership to get $400 on my old Beetle as a trade-in on the new, $1900 1963 Beetle. I did not want to get into debt and be paying interest, so I used most of my nest egg to buy the VW outright. I sold it 14 years later for $470. For the two years we lived in Wisconsin, this was our only car. On days when it was my turn to drive to work in the carpool, Sue would journey to her job by bus. As a result, we could afford to live on my salary as an engineer and save all of Sue's salary as an occupational therapist. We bought our first house 18 months later. The VW was also our only car in Massachusetts, as Sue was now a stay-at-home mom. We decided we would forgo the convenience of owning a second car until we could pay for it in cash. We did so in September 1967, buying a new Buick LeSabre, a safer car for our growing family. But we still had the VW as our second car for ten more years.

I replaced the VW with a new Toyota Celica in 1977. I drove it for eight years before giving it to my son for his last two years at the Air Force Academy. We bought Sue a new Toyota Supra in 1980, which she drove until giving it to our daughter in 1985 for her freshman year at Cal Poly San Luis Obispo. We paid cash for each car we owned, with one exception. In December 2001 we bought Sue a year-old Jaguar S-Type from a dealer, who had certified it with a six-year warranty Jaguar offered a financial incentive: 1.9% interest, provided we paid it off in 24 monthly payments. We accepted it since I was unable to negotiate a cash rebate in lieu of the financing deal. At least Sue earned a high FICO credit score by satisfying the regular payment schedule.

I did not have to worry about my car when I became general manager of the Intermetrics Aerospace Systems Group in 1985, because the company leased a new Chrysler New Yorker (my choice) for me every three years. They also paid for the insurance, gasoline, car washes, and maintenance. My only expense was the income tax on the percentage of time for personal use. When I left the company in 1993, I bought the 1992 New Yorker for the residual value ($15,000). I drove it for ten years and 110,000 miles, selling it to a private party in 2001 for $4,500.

I bought my first Lexus, a new GS 300, in November 2000. I had retired July 1, 1999 and spent the next 17 months test driving almost every sport luxury sedan until finally making my decision. I loved the car (Yes, I let emotion influence the decision.) and sold it to a private party ten years later. Only after I sold it, did I buy my new Lexus LS 460. I planned to drive it for ten years also, and bought the extended warranty based on this plan. I believe that over the last 55 years had I not kept my cars for such an extended length of time and paid cash for them, we could not afford the great cars we now own, unless I continued to work well into this millennium.

One more benefit of keeping the car a long time: fewer times in dealing with the problem of selling the old car.

Why not lease or buy on time?

Interest on debt can be a slow drain on financial resources. In addition, it carries a risk that if one experiences a major unexpected expense or loses his job, the repercussions could be devastating. Moreover, the interest on an auto loan is not deductible. The Lexus dealer offered to finance my car at an exceptionally low 6.5% rate. To break even, I would have to invest the cash at approximately 10%, assuming the IRS and California would tax it at ordinary income. I do not know of any investment that would guarantee 10% with no risk to the principle. Leasing is even worse. Not only would I be paying the embedded interest in up-front and monthly payments, but also the lender's embedded fees and profit. In addition, there is risk that I could owe more at the end of the lease, depending on the mileage and car condition.

Kurth Krause

Why not trade in the old car, instead of selling it yourself?

Selling your old car can be a pain. First, you must get the car looking good, and keep it clean. Then you must set a proper price and advertise. You must be on hand when people call to show the car. You must put up with "low-ballers" who offer a rock bottom price, hoping you are getting desperate, so they can resell it at a real profit. You may have to negotiate, as some third-party buyers will not initially offer your asking price. You must demand cash because even a cashier's check can be forged. Then, after the sale, there is a risk of being hounded if something goes wrong with the car. (They know your phone number and where you live.)

But the benefit is economic. A car dealer, or a wholesaler such as CarMax, will offer several thousand dollars under the car's value. They will then spruce it up and sell it for a nice profit. To understand what a dealer is truly offering, it is necessary to get a final price on the new car you intend to buy to avoid confusing the two deals (e.g., high price on the new car offset by high trade-in price). I sold my ten-year-old Chrysler for $4,500 when the dealer would give me only $1,000 on a trade-in. We sold Sue's Chrysler Town and Country for $3,000 more than the dealer's offer. I sold my 2001 Lexus GS 300 for $4,000 more than the CarMax price and $2,000 over the best trade-in offer.

What do I have to do to sell the old car myself?

Obviously, the used car must look its best; no one wants to buy a shabby-looking car. Also, it should be in good mechanical condition. The seller could be liable for not disclosing a known mechanical problem. The tradeoff comes in the cost to prep the car. I sold my 2001 Lexus without spending the estimated 1,000 it would cost to professionally repair all the dings and scratches, including one tiny dent on the trunk. I believed that I was more likely to sell it at a $1,000 discount (I reduced the asking price accordingly.) than to fix them perfectly. Instead, I bought a vial of matching touch-up paint from the Lexus dealer and carefully painted them. They were still noticeable, but small compared to the overall paint job, which still had its new-car luster.

Next step is to determine the asking price. I used the *edmunds.com* website to determine this. In addition to basing the price on the options and mileage, it guides the user as to how to accurately assess the condition. It computes the *True Value* (Edmunds' assessment based on comparable other sales) for the sale by dealer, by private party, and blue book value. In addition, it provides asking prices on comparable cars currently advertised. I have learned how important it is to get the pricing right. When I first set the price for my used Lexus at $9,500, I received only two serious calls in the first week. When I reduced it to $7,500, I received many more, including seven calls after I sold the car.

Then, after gathering all the information necessary to describe the car (It pays to have saved the original window sticker.), you are ready to place an ad. The best place is no longer the newspapers. I spent $168 for a small two-week ad in the Orange County Register and received no calls from it. I paid $59 for an ad in Autotrader.com (linked from Edmunds) that remains online until the car sells. It also is carried in the weekly Autotrader publication for no additional charge. I received at least ten serious responses from this. Autotrader allows up to 12 photographs of the car as well as plenty of room for the online description in detail. You can change the online data as often as you wish. The hard copy publication is much more restrictive with only one photo and few words.

Be prepared to negotiate. You need to know how much you are willing to come down when someone makes an offer. How fast you want to sell and the prices your competition is asking should determine this. I probably accepted the offer on my first Lexus too quickly, based on the calls I received afterward. Sue sold her ten-year-old Jaguar in 2010 using the Auto Trader for $2,000 more than the trade-in price. She then bought a new Jaguar on December 31, 2000, using the leverage of the last day of the year to successfully negotiate. Ten years later she sold this Jag for $10,000 to the same person who bought her previous one.

I sold my ten-year-old Lexis LS 460 for $20,900 cash. I advertised on Autotrader for three weeks. Once again, I realized $4,000 more than offered by the Lexus dealer or CarMax. I sold it two weeks before my new Tesla Model S was delivered in March 2017. Tesla does not negotiate price, so I had to pay Manufacturer's Suggested Retail Price (MSRP).

Try to meet with the prospective buyer away from your house. Take your possessions out of the glove compartment and car pockets, especially identification information. Had the wise bird mentioned this, it would have saved me a hassle after the buyer drove off with my car and contents.

How should I buy a new car today?

First, sell your old car. Yes, it could put you without a car for a short time (You could always rent or use Uber or Lyft during this period, if necessary.), but it is a problem if you are trying to sell the old one after you have taken possession of the new one. Which one are you going to leave outside the garage; the one you want to keep clean to sell or your brand-new purchase? Also, this would create more pressure to get rid of it, maybe at a lower price. Of course, you must continue to pay insurance on both.

But before you advertise the old one, do all the homework necessary to be ready to buy the new one. Know the exact options and color you want and whether your dealer(s) have it on hand. Negotiate the price close to your final offer, so that when you are ready (after you've sold the old car), you can comfortably make your final bid, and have a good idea what they will accept.

Go to *edmunds.com* to determine their recommendation as to the proper price, then see if you can beat it. The website provides the MSRP (sticker price), the factory invoice (the price the dealer paid), and the *True Value* (the average actual price paid by others). If the dealers have an inventory of your car on hand and they have not been selling well, you may be able to negotiate a price near the factory invoice (try within $500). However, if the car is in demand and the dealers cannot keep it in stock, the best price may be close to MSRP. Edmunds' *True Value* is a good indicator for this. But you can beat the *True Value* price with some effort since this is an average. Prices are always lower near the end of the sales year (usually October) when the next year's cars start arriving and crowding their lots. Sometimes you can get a better price at the end (or beginning) of the month when the salesmen are trying to meet their quotas.

Once you know exactly what you want, you can use the Internet to get price quotes from multiple dealers. In theory, this bypasses the salesman and his commission, but you are just trading his commission for that of the Internet sales manager at the dealer. Another way is to get a Costco price. They have a business relationship with a dealer from almost every make of car. They put you in touch with that dealer and, in theory, he gives you his lowest, non-negotiable price. But I have found this price is also negotiable. By getting a low-price quote, you can save a lot of gamesmanship on the part of the salesmen by asking them to beat your lowest quoted price. Otherwise they will string you along by slowly lowering their highest price, involving iterations with their sales manager. Most of this gaming is false, just trying to get you to go for a high price that increases their commission. Persistence and patience usually work. Sue bought her new 1980 Supra within $50 of our target price by spending six hours at the dealer, never backing down from her price, and calling me periodically to play their game by having me saying no. By applying all these techniques, I reduced the price of my LS 460 (a car in reasonably high demand) by $5,000 under MSRP. It took time, but I think it was worth it. Without the techniques, the dealer's "special price" to me was $3,500 higher. It is also possible to negotiate the extras (e.g. extended warranty, protective coating) that the finance guy tries to sell you after completing your negotiations with the salesman.

So, my 56 years of experience with cars have taught me: keep your old car until you have the cash to pay for the new one; avoid emotional decisions; do your homework; and shop around. A little effort can save major dollars in the long run. (These techniques can also work with purchasing expensive items, such as appliances, electronics, and furniture.)

The Future

I predict that in the future some of the above advice may no longer be relevant. The electric vehicles (EVs) will replace the internal combustion engine (ICE) cars. This may take longer for the lower price cars than the luxury cars because of the higher price of most EVs, such as Tesla, but I would not buy a new ICE, ever. The EV will eventually dominate, especially when they have been certified for self-driving. They are already the safest car on the road, avoiding accidents that humans do not. The insurance claims will drop precipitously, driving down insurance premiums. But more importantly, maintenance and repair costs will be near zero, as is my current Tesla. (No oil changes, no points, no spark plugs, no tune-ups, and no radiators or hoses.) However, I found their tire wear to be expensive. Their instant torque and acceleration cannot be beat which may account for the short tire longevity. Electric charging is 67% cheaper than gasoline. Their range between charging is growing longer (310 miles for the Tesla Model 3, 620 miles for the upcoming 2021 Roadster). And they are continuously being improved at no cost to the owner via software downloads from the factory. But because no one will be buying new ICE cars, the price of used ICE cars will be cheaper.

7. HEALTH IS VITAL

It took me a long time to accept that health is more important than money. My youth and excellent health deterred me from listening to elders who dwelt over and over on the importance of health. I suppose I needed to experience health challenges before I gradually accepted the premise that if you lose your health, no amount of money can compensate.

Smoking

I did learn that cigarette smoking was hazardous to my heath, but I was hooked. I tried to quit 100 times, but succumbed. I smoked almost one pack per day for 17 years. I took a test to learn why I smoked which revealed I did so because I enjoyed it. This was certainly the worst motivation to give them up. I finally quit thanks to my children. I first gave it up at home, attempting to not upset them. But they figured out I was smoking at work. So, they found the pack in my glove compartment and poked holes in the cigarettes. I finally was able to quit and have not smoked a cigarette since 1997. (But I still like the smell if someone lights up.) My sister did not quit and died of lung cancer at age 73.

Al least I had the good sense to exercise regularly at a gym: 35 minutes of aerobics and 20 minutes of muscle maintenance with weight machines. As I entered my fifties, I started gaining weight, mostly in my stomach. I gained 40 pounds over my college weight. It could have been a lot worse without the aerobics.

Surgery

I should have taken the advice that neglecting dental hygiene can produce regrets later in life. I brushed only once per day and rarely flossed. This resulted in periodontal disease, requiring painful surgical scaling and curettage more than once to keep from losing my teeth. I required several molar extractions which were not fun. I had four expensive dental implants.

I had problems with pain in my shoulders, requiring bilateral rotator cuff surgery, including reattaching a tendon to the bone. It took six months before I could play golf again. Had I sought treatment earlier when the pain just started, I might have avoided surgery altogether.

I developed carpal tunnel syndrome in my right wrist. I should have gotten a second opinion instead of plunging ahead with wrist fusion surgery that gave me 35% loss of motion and 30% loss of strength and adversely affected my golf after a year of rehabilitation. I never did regain full dexterity, and I still experience some residual pain.

Vision

Like so many other people my age, I developed cataracts in both eyes. But I should have checked out the ophthalmologist's track record, rather than just relying on his several degrees before I agreed to the surgery. I had worn glasses, then contact lenses for 40 years when I went to Dr. Sadri. He assured me that if I elected to have expensive multifocal lenses implanted after he removed the cataracts, I would be able to see my golf ball land as well as read small print. (Advice from the wise bird would have saved me from some real problems.) I had been nearsighted, able to read well, but not see distance well, even with my glasses. (I was developing macular degeneration, so had switched from contacts to prescription sunglasses, which I would have to wear outdoors forever.) So, Sadri convinced me to spend the $5,400 per lens to achieve this result.

But the highly credentialed ophthalmologist was a charlatan. He did not explain that the new lenses would not correct my substantial astigmatism. So, after the implants, I could not see the golf ball at a distance. Dr. Sadri said he could fix the problem with Lasik surgery. He was incompetent. After the Lasik, I was legally blind in my right eye for almost six months. Sadri must have received a kickback from the lens manufacturer because he could have inserted lenses to correct for the astigmatism that were much less costly. I finally got a second opinion who told me that nothing could be done now, but the Lasik procedure should never have been attempted. I considered suing Sadri but realized that my macular degeneration would complicate any lawsuit. Today with glasses, my eyesight is 20/40 just barely sufficient to pass a driver's test.

Vital Organs

Last year I had a heart valve replacement. The surgeon went through my femoral artery and inserted a new valve into the defective aortic valve arthroscopically. The next day I went home. One week later I played in a golf tournament. I am amazed at what the medical profession can do with our bodies today. Seeing my chest in a 3D ultrasound reinforced my admiration of the amazing design of the human body.

Sue's family has a history of kidney disease. Her father was on dialysis for eight years before he died. Therefore, she had regular checkups with her nephrologist, who turned out to be incompetent. Over the years, he repeatedly told her that although her kidneys were not perfect, she would not need dialysis until she was well into her 80s. At age 69, he told her that her kidneys were failing, and she needed to start dialysis, but she was too old to get on the national transplant list. We immediately fired the incompetent doctor and were referred to an excellent nephrologist, Dr. Sawhney. He determined that she did not need to start dialysis yet, but he would monitor her closely. He referred her to UCLA to apply for a kidney, but they estimated the wait at ten years.

No one from our immediate family qualified as a donor because we all had the wrong blood type. But a 69-year-old friend volunteered. He had Sue's blood type, but UCLA threatened to disqualify him due to his age. When he argued that he was fit for his age, they relinquished and began testing him. He passed every test and was a good match until they found he had one too many arteries and veins attached to his kidneys and rejected him as a donor. But we learned about a nonprofit website *MatchingDonors.com*. I wrote a piece on why Sue deserved a kidney, found my favorite picture of her, and submitted them along with the required $600 to get on their website. Almost immediately we received responses from six potential donors with matching blood type. UCLA rejected the first two because they were outside the United States. UCLA said we would pay to get them here, and we would never see them again after they arrived.

We were priming Sue for dialysis as her kidneys were now declining dangerously. The surgeon was preparing to implant a catheter in her stomach for at-home peritoneal dialysis. We had a home visit by a nurse to show us how to perform it three times per week.

But the third Matching Donors response from a 25-year-old man from Oklahoma seemed like a possibility. Robert said he wanted to donate because his grandmother died of kidney disease. After submitting his blood sample, UCLA invited him to undertake testing. So, we arranged to fly him to California but also contacted the fourth potential donor as a backup. UCLA's tests showed a 98% match. So, after taking Robert to see almost every venue in our area (He had never been outside Oklahoma.), he went home to wait for the UCLA decision. We paid him for everything we legally could: his expenses, wages, etc. (The website warns that buying or selling a kidney results in a $5,000 fine and five years in prison.)

The hospital invited him back to do the transplant. Again, we were concerned he might back out. This time he came out with his cousin for support. Once again, I took them to the Hollywood Walk of Fame and Rodeo Drive (their choices) before the surgery. We flew a flag of Oklahoma, which Robert claimed was flown over the state capitol to commemorate the transplant. But first, the UCLA head nephrologist grilled him one-on-one on how much money I was paying him for this, causing him to cry.

Robert came through. Our son flew out for the surgery and encouraged him. The doctors suggested postponing the catheter surgery because the transplant was imminent. I witnessed his kidney begin doing its wonderful job in Sue. They were prepared to carry out a dialysis during the surgery if necessary, as Sue's kidneys were functioning at only 5%. So, the transplant occurred just in time. After recuperating at our home and again reimbursing him for all allowable expenses, he flew home. He is now a member of the family, as Sue sends him presents for holidays just as she does for our children.

Covid-19

I do not have any unique words of wisdom about dealing with the Covid-19 pandemic. But I must address it here because it is such a threat for us. At Reata Glen, we are under stringent rules to minimize the risk because all the residents are in the high-risk category: over 60 years of age, many with underlying conditions that make us more vulnerable. Since Sue takes anti-immune medication to prevent rejection of her kidney, she must be especially careful. Currently, July 1, we are beginning to relax the restrictions; we are now able to dine at the RG restaurants but must observe social distancing at all times and wear face masks except when we are seated at the table. The restrictions are working since we have no cases among either the residents or the staff. I will be happy when they reopen the fitness center and the poker tables.

8. CHOICE OF HOBBIES CAN ENHANCE LIFE

Golf

My career gave me great satisfaction. However, I needed enjoyable activities outside my time at work. Initially golf filled this perfectly. Golf might be the best of all participative sports. Psychologist and successful author M. Scott Peck (*The Road Less Traveled,* et al) declared it so in his book, *Golf and the Spirit.* Peck, once an expert amateur tennis player, got bored with tennis when he could not find anyone who could beat him. He took up golf in his late thirties and never mastered the game. (He rarely broke 100.) He stated in tennis there were 30 different types of shots to learn–in golf there must be 10,000. He claimed the next best games were likely chess and bridge, but they were a distant second. He makes the point that golf displays a person's character. The frustration of a bad shot can produce a volley of expletives or even club throwing, or it can demonstrate patience, honesty, and integrity. The rules of golf call for the golfer to call any infraction on himself and announce it, while penalizing himself with the appropriate number of strokes. A true golfer will always do so.

If the game is so hard, why is it so addictive? Even the pros say they average, perhaps, six perfect shots per round. (Of course, their "imperfect" shots are rather good.) And it takes many hours of practice on the driving range before a beginner can finally hit that one near-perfect shot–very frustrating! I think the fact that one cannot play it perfectly is one of the big attractions. Once one does hit that (near) perfect shot in the "sweet spot" of the club and feel the ball compress, it feels as if the ball was almost not there. This first good shot makes the game addictive. One feels that he/she can now hit all shots that way, or at least should be able to do so. Some describe the feeling as orgasmic. So, we spend the rest of our lives trying to hit them all perfectly.

If we hit several good shots in a row, we now believe we have found the secret and will never play badly again. But by the next round we have lost it again and want to quit the game. But we never do. In reference to the good swing, it is said we never own it, but only rent it. Perhaps that is why we remember our best rounds forever–they are so rare.

I grew up playing without learning the proper swing–a major mistake. My dad (who never broke 100) took me to play my first time and bet me I would "whiff" (swing and totally miss the ball) at least ten times in the 18 holes. I took that bet. After all, how hard would it be to hit a ball that was not moving? I played baseball and could sometimes hit a pitched ball traveling at more than 80 miles per hour and curving or hopping. Well, I won the bet. I **only** whiffed eight times. At age 14 I started playing with my friends during summer vacation at the local public courses. On weekdays, we would ride our bikes to the course to get there at sunrise to tee off by 6 a.m. We had to complete the round in time to sign up for another 18 holes before noon. The Milwaukee County courses allowed kids under age 16 to play for 35 cents on weekdays provided we bought our permits before noon.

But I never had a lesson as a child, and have been paying the price ever since, trying to correct the many flaws ingrained in those early years. I wish someone (the wise bird) had advised me to take up golf instead of baseball in high school so that I would have received some instruction on the proper swing. We could not afford and did not even think of paying for lessons in those days. We did not even practice at a driving range. Most of the Milwaukee County courses did not have a range. So, we had fun hacking away with our flawed swings and typically scored 120-140 for 18 holes those first years. I remember telling my buddies that I was determined on that particular day to not score higher than a six on any hole on the back nine. I succeeded. I scored nine straight sixes! By the time I was in college, I had been able to break 100 several times; my best score on the relatively easy county courses was 91. Then I met a real golfer.

I was 19 when I met Sue, a pretty, petite coed, on the student train to the Rose Bowl of 1960, I learned she was a golfer. Her family belonged to South Hills, a private country club in Fond du Lac, Wisconsin. We started dating and she invited me to play South Hills that summer. She beat me like a drum and continued to beat me regularly through our courtship and early married years on every course we played. Her father had been a scratch golfer, taught her until she was ten, then turned her over to a pro for lessons. As a teenager, she was winning girls' golf tournaments throughout the state. She did not hit it far, but she did hit it straight. I could out-drive her by 50 yards, but it usually produced a big slice, well into the rough, woods, or water.

As a sophomore at Wisconsin, one of my fraternity brothers invited 20 of us to play golf at Olympia Fields in Chicago and spend the night in his gigantic home south of Chicago. I was so impressed by the course (where the previous year the PGA Championship Tournament was played). The majestic clubhouse was even more impressive. It had seven bars and two giant men's locker rooms with full poker tables every 20 feet between the lockers. Each of us had our own caddies. Mine was an "ancient" 40-year-old. I felt like Arnold Palmer walking up the 18th fairway, my caddie carrying my clubs. I made up my mind that this was my lifetime goal, to join a club like Olympia Fields.

Finally, at age 27, we joined an unpretentious private club after we moved to Texas, and I took lessons from our club pro. I learned why golf is so hard. It is imperative to develop confidence in each shot, especially the putt, but at the same time one must concentrate intensely on the shot. But concentration can hinder confidence. My handicap quickly dropped to a 19, then gradually worked its way down to a 14, and I was occasionally beating Sue. I was hitting my drives on the hard Texas turf up to 270 yards, surprising most, including myself. I remember winning the Flag Tournament July 4, 1973, with my 14 handicap. Up to that time I had never broken 80; my best nine-hole score was 39. But this day was different. I chipped in for a birdie on the first hole, the toughest one on the course. I got "in a zone" and made the turn at 33, three under par! I parred the 10th hole, the 2nd most difficult hole on the course, but the pressure got to me, finishing with a 76, but good enough to easily win the tournament.

When we moved to California, we joined Mesa Verde Country Club with a great golf course. We bought our house so close to the course that we could walk there. Since all four of us were playing at least once per week, the $80 monthly dues were less than we would pay for public course green fees. When I sold my membership 44 years later and I was the only one in our family playing, the dues were more than $1200 per month.

MVCC grew in stature while I was there. In the early days we hosted five PGA tournaments, won by such notables as Billy Casper. Tony Lema, who was the third best professional golfer in the world when he died in a plane crash in 1966, won his first PGA tournament at Mesa Verde in 1962. He bought champagne for the press and earned the nickname "Champagne Tony." We hosted six LPGA tournaments from 1979-1986, won twice by Nancy Lopez. We hosted the inaugural Toshiba Classic for the PGA seniors at Mesa Verde in 1995. Tiger Woods played his first private course there at age six, shooting 98 from the **back tees**. Tiger raised over $1 million for the Tiger Woods Foundation at each of the amateur tournaments he sponsored at Mesa Verde. I was in my final year of my six years on the Board of Directors during his first one. He and Freddy Couples gave a clinic before the tournament. As a member of the board, I had my picture taken with Tiger, had him autograph golf caps for my grandchildren and, with Sue, attended his block party at the Grove in Anaheim.

As our kids started approaching the age to learn golf, I made up my mind that they would learn the correct technique and not have to suffer, as I did, correcting the flaws. At age six, Scott played in a three-hole tournament and finished first among the 6-8-year-old kids with something like 24 strokes. He won a trophy and was hooked. Sheryl was not as enamored with the game. By the time we moved to California when Scott was ten and Sheryl eight, we had to drag her out on Sundays to fill out the family foursome. It was not until she was 14 and starting high school that Sheryl really got interested in the game–or maybe it was interest in the boys who played the game. She tried out for the Estancia High School boys' team (they had no girls' team in the 1980's) and was one of the top five players. Scott was captain of the team his junior and senior years. Sheryl says she still has men ask her, "Weren't you Sheryl Krause? I remember you beating me at the *whatsoever* tournament in high school." Sheryl, like her mother, never hits the ball far but has a soft touch around the greens. I remember the first time she beat me for nine holes at Pinehurst #9 when she was 13. At age 17 she won the girls' club championship, succeeding perpetual champion Kim Saiki (who later was an LPGA pro for two decades). Sheryl played in the junior circuit throughout Southern California against others who also became pros. We took her to Hawaii after her high school graduation in 1985, where she shot 77 on Mauna Lani the first time that she saw the course. She spent the rest of the time on the beach, declaring she was not going to play any more since she could not do better than 77. Her handicap was nine at the time. She now plays only once per year (with me in our club's father-daughter tournament), but still hits the ball straight. She always beats her husband who hits the ball 50 yards farther than I do.

Scott successfully tried out for the golf team at the Air Force Academy. He played collegiate golf for them for all four years. He was particularly happy to make the traveling team his freshman year because it allowed him to skip the harassment heaped on the freshmen (doolies) by the upperclassmen of his squadron at each meal. Instead, during the spring and fall quarters he dined with his golf team. His team traveled to Florida each spring quarter, playing many great courses as a precursor to the intercollegiate events. I remember the middle of his freshman year, the first time he was permitted to come home. We played golf together both Saturday and Sunday. He had to give me seven strokes because of my 12 handicap. On Saturday, we played from the regular men's tees as I usually do, being not a long hitter. I shot my second-best round ever with a 75, winning $3. Scott, being a long hitter, challenged me on Sunday to play from the championship tees, which are almost 500 yards longer. I shot 76 (my best from the long tees); another $3. He avowed he would never give me strokes again. My handicap dropped three strokes the next month to a nine, my career low. (Later that year, I shot my career best round, a 73: 16 pars and two bogies.) I had my only hole-in-one in 1989. Sue has had two holes-in-one, just two years apart. Scott and I won the MVCC Member-Guest Derby Tournament in 2014.

I have fond memories of playing with Scott and Sue's father, Arnold Firle, whenever we would visit her parents in Fond du Lac in the summer and Scottsdale in the winter. I loved his course in Fond du Lac–a par-71 with a unique back nine: a par-three followed by eight consecutive par-four holes. Sue and I had our wedding reception at South Hills in 1963. Arnie's course in Arizona, Rio Verde, had less character, but I loved the quiet setting, being bordered by the Tonto National Forest.

Soon after I met Arnie, I followed him around for the final 18 holes in the South Hills match-play club championship. He had made the finals by beating the club's up-coming 18-year-old star on Saturday. But the finals required walking 36 holes, optionally using a caddie. At the time I thought it extraordinary that a 50-year-old could walk 36 holes. He played the finals on Sunday against one of his cronies: a 36-year-old. They were tied after the first 18. Arnie was one down going into the 34th hole, the most difficult par-4 on the course. He made a miraculous par to even the match and went to the 36th tee tied. His second shot on this par-4 was well left of the green in the high rough, while his opponent was on the fringe of the green in two. Arnie took a long time looking over the shot, then, using his "equalizer" (a sand wedge), hit an amazing clutch shot to three feet from the hole. His opponent's putt lipped the cup, leaving it 2½ feet away. But the cup was cut on a crown, so Arnie took his time looking it over before holing the putt. His opponent took almost no time–and missed! Arnie was the club champion for the fourth time. He was now my hero.

At age 80 he was still playing golf, but then held a 13 handicap when he started dialysis because of his failed kidneys. He responded to an invitation for a charity tournament in Wisconsin to benefit combating kidney disease. His foursome of doctors was astounded when they learned he was a patient–the only patient on dialysis in the tournament. They did not win, but Arnie was their star, leading their foursome, hole after hole. Arnie continued to play golf until he was 86. In his lifetime he had several holes-in-one, served as president of his club, and had worked his way up from caddie to the best golfer at his club. His heroes were Ben Hogan and Arnold Palmer. He died at age 88.

Arnie proved to me that golf is the best lifetime game. Few 80-year-olds can play a sport their entire lifetime. It is truly the sport of a lifetime, and the sooner we learn the swing correctly, the more enjoyable it will be the rest of our lives, even if we cannot hit the perfect shot each time. When I sold my membership at MVCC at age 79 I was still playing golf 2-3 times per week,

I am not sure I would recommend team sports because their value is limited for lifetime enjoyment. Many of us choose a team sport early in life. It can develop great social skills. We need to make friends early in life. Team sports enable such opportunities. However, many of us, including me, do not think of the lifelong implications of choosing a sport. Even those who excel in a sport do not think about whether that sport is something that will be of real value to us after we graduate from high school or college. How many of the top high school athletes in a team sport are benefiting from what they learned? Some, if they are top athletes in high school, may be able to get an athletic scholarship to college. But few can continue in their later years.

Kurth Krause

Contract Bridge

After I retired, a friend suggested taking up competitive duplicate bridge. I used to play when I was in my 20s but dropped it to concentrate on my career. I had forgotten how much fun it is. But I had much to learn because the bidding had become much more sophisticated and complex. He gave me a software program to learn more than a dozen conventions, wherein bids mean something quite different from how they sounded. Of course, it is imperative that you and your partner know exactly what these bids mean. Also, I had to fill out a convention card and make it available to our opponents. In addition, I must explain the meaning of my partner's previous bid(s), if the opponents asked.

What makes duplicate bridge so much fun is that every pair facing the same orientation (East-West, or North-South) plays the same hands. So, the luck of having great or bad hands is eliminated. All that matters is whether your result is better than the others with the same hand. For most bridge clubs, it takes approximately four hours to play a session. You need to enjoy the game to put in this investment in time. And it costs money to play. The card fees pay for the venue, the director, and the national organization which tabulates the results. Today the charge is at least $10 per session, depending on the club. So, what is the reward? Masterpoints. For a typical session playing against eight-ten opponent pairs, the winner receives 1.5 masterpoints, which are recorded by the national governing body, a member of the World Bridge Federation. In North America this is the America Contract Bridge League, which has a current membership of 165,000.

The ACBL collects annual dues from each member in addition to a portion of the card fees from each club event. The ACBL, which is non-profit corporation, provides an excellent instructional website, publishes a monthly magazine, organizes regional and national tournaments, and keeps track of the number of masterpoints won by each member. It also identifies the rank held by each member, from a Junior Master with at least five points, to a Life Master with at least 500 points, to a Grand Life Master with at least 10,000 points. The higher rankings of Life Master and above require "pigmented" masterpoints earned in higher level tournaments. Currently, I have 1,460 points and hold the rank of Silver Life Master. Sue, who began soon after I, has 580 points and holds the rank of Bronze Life Master.

Poker

When we retired and moved to Reata Glen, three poker games caught my interest in the clubhouse billiard room. There are two beautiful poker tables; each can accommodate up to nine players. I bought and read three books on how to play poker, recommendations from my friend Richard Kallmann, a professional poker player. I learned there was more to the game than just luck, but the strategies are complex and not easy to master. But it is not necessary to become an expert at Reata Glen since the stakes are low. The maximum bet is 25 cents. It is rare to win or lose more than $10 in a two-hour session.

But I thoroughly enjoy it. The Monday and Wednesday night games are open to any resident. "Dealer's choice" enables a variety of games, including wild cards. But the Tuesday night game is more serious: Texas Hold'em and Seven Card Stud with no wild cards are almost exclusively chosen by the dealer. The game is by invitation only, and more fun for me. We even plan future tournaments with a $20 entry fee, no-limit betting, and World Championship of Poker rules.

During the Covid-19 pandemic, because we are sheltered-in-place, Sue and I renewed two other two-handed card games: Gin Rummy and Cribbage.

Music

Music has always been an important part of my life. As a child, my parents encouraged me to play an instrument. They convinced me to take lessons on a borrowed, sub-sized accordion at age five. But, a year later when I was ready for a real full-sized accordion, they could not afford it. I really wanted to learn how to play the piano, but that would be impossible. To this day, the piano has always been my favorite instrument. I enjoy listening to piano solos, be they classical or pop songs.

When I was 14, I took guitar lessons, but Elvis Presley had not yet hit the scene. The popularity of the guitar seduced the teens only after I gave it up. The little wise bird should have told me to continue, and it might have been satisfying for the rest of my life. I did acquire a set of bongo drums in college and played often with another fraternity brother. But eventually they wore out and I never replaced them.

So, I became an aficionado of recorded music. As a pre-teen, I remember spending hours in the basement listening to my father's vinyl 78 RPMs on the Victrola player. In 1938 Benny Goodman's orchestra, including Harry James on trumpet, Goodman on clarinet, and Gene Krupa on drums, performed a famous jazz concert in Carnegie Hall. My father owned a 1950 copy of Goodman's *Sing, Sing, Sing* played at the concert, which became my favorite. I probably wore it out, listening to it. I became a fan of the old Big Bands.

My favorite recording artists became Johnny Mathis and Barbara Streisand. I can always get out of a funky mood by listening to their music and many others on the Tesla streaming music service. It is so cool to call up the song and artist of my choice and listen while driving. Maybe I should have switched my double major to geology and astronomy. Then I could have been a rock star.

I also loved musical theater. My grandfather treated us to attend the musical production of *Oklahoma* in Milwaukee when I was seven years old. I was enthralled and in love with musical plays ever since. When I was 20, two fraternity brothers and I visited New York City for the first time, on our way to an Alpha Delta Phi national convention in Amherst, Massachusetts. We bought tickets for the French musical *Irma La Duce* and the blockbuster *The Sound of Music* starring Mary Martin. I was hooked!

When I was president of the fraternity, we performed an original musical skit, *Emancipation Proclamation,* for Wisconsin's annual Humorology Contest with Delta Gamma sorority. Our Stan Storasta, majoring in linguistics, and one of the most gifted people I have ever met, wrote all three original songs and much of the play. I still remember the songs 58 years later. They were Broadway quality. At the time, the Wisconsin campus was exploding in population: 18,000 students my freshman year; 30,000 four years later. So, our theme became the crowded campus. At the top of Bascom Hill in the middle of the campus, is a prominently displayed statue of Abraham Lincoln seated in a large chair. The female students did not cross in front of him, because legend had it that if ever a virgin walked in front of Lincoln, he would stand. (Remember, this was 1961.). This, in part, added to the crowding at the top of the hill. Our skit depicted a boy and girl admiring each other from afar but were inhibited from meeting due to the congestion. The three scenes of the skit included numerous jokes about campus crowding. But in Scene Three, the girl walked in front of the Lincoln statue to meet the boy, and Lincoln (our 6'8" basketball player) stood, forever relieving the crowded conditions on Bascom Hill. We were all disappointed when we didn't win but took second place. I regretted that I had not joined the cast, enhancing my memories of this great time of original musical theater.

Spectator Sports

I was never much of an athlete but became a rabid fan of pro sports. In 1953, the Braves, the first major league team to relocate in 50 years, moved from Boston to Milwaukee. That was a big deal for the city. There were only 16 big-league baseball teams at that time. My grandfather had season seats right behind the catcher: Box 1, Row 1, Seats 1 and 2. He took me to see several games, where I could judge how much stuff the pitcher had on the ball. (I was a pitcher in high school.) Each year from 1953 until I went to college in 1958, I had a ticket to the Braves opening-day game and my high school allowed me to attend. I became such a rabid fan that I knew the batting average of every player in the National League and the earned-run average of every pitcher. In 1954 I personally attended 54 of the 76 home games, either with my grandfather, my uncles, or my friends. I had fond memories of Warren Spahn's 300th win, Joe Adcock's four home runs and a double in a single game, and Eddie Mathew's game winning home run in the tenth inning of Game Four of the 1957 World Series, beating the New York Yankees. But when the owner of the Braves moved the team to Atlanta, where he made more money from TV rights, than in Milwaukee, where the average attendance had been 1.5 million per year (280,000 their last year in Boston), I suddenly lost all interest in baseball.

But I have always been a strong Green Bay Packers fan. Everyone who grew up in Wisconsin is. It is the only team "owned" by the fans in that many own one share of the stock in the team with no monetary value. The Packers have won more national championships than any other team: nine pre-Super Bowl NFL titles and four Super Bowl victories. But with their three Hall-of-Fame quarterbacks: Bart Starr, Brett Favre, and Arron Rodgers, they are exciting to watch, win or lose.

OF course, watching my Wisconsin Badgers play football has always been a great hobby. Sue and I saw them lose in the 1960 Rose Bowl. Later we saw them win their next three Rose Bowl games against the Pac Ten champions.

Bowling

My maternal grandfather owned a small, four-lane bowling alley in Milwaukee. His sons (my uncles) were good bowlers. As a child, sometimes on Saturdays my uncle would let me score the games bowled by their two teams and pay me with cokes and candy bars. One uncle, Gene Raffel, became nationally ranked, averaging 234 one year in sanctioned matches. He twice won the state championship and was inducted into the Milwaukee Hall of Fame in 1977. He and my two distant cousins held the world's record for decades as a three-man team: 2404 with an 859-single game.

Sue and I bowled in a league in Texas for six years but were never particularly good. I averaged 150; she averaged 130. Bowling can be a fun sport but currently not especially popular in California.

Kurth Krause

The Media and Books

Recently, I have learned not to trust much of the news media due to their obvious bias and motivation to promote a progressive political ideology and sensationalize information, rather than reporting factually and accurately. As a result, I have cancelled my subscription to the LA Times in favor of the Wall Street Journal. I also no longer watch CNN News, which used to be my favorite network for watching balanced news reports, but no longer. Also, I no longer trust the Internet for factual information, having learned about "fake news." first-hand.

I have always enjoyed reading, as a child as well as an adult. My bookshelves are stocked with self-help books, including bridge, investing, golf, poker, and blackjack, as well as history, biographies, space travel, and several novels. I learned to be selective with authors who write novels. In my opinion, the books of best-selling authors are sometimes not professionally created. I never enjoyed a David Baldacci novel, but always liked John Grisham's novels. I also listen to audio books while working out at the fitness center. Overall, these books have enhanced my knowledge and enabled more informed decision-making.

After my freshman year in college I wanted to read about esoteric phenomena in the universe. I found a library copy of *Relativity for the Layman* by Albert Einstein. I believed I was certainly ready for this, having completed two semesters of calculus and modern physics. It was only 25 pages and the first page was enticing text. But my high self-esteem was brought back to earth when I found the other 24 pages were nothing but partial differential equations, belying the title.

My grandson, Griffin, is a voracious reader, as is evident by his in-depth knowledge on so many topics. At age 16, he once read 40 books in six months.

Writing

I do not know if this is classified as a hobby, since I am earning money from my book sales, but not on the same earning level as my aerospace career. However, I always was serious about my writing. I realized that I had a knack for it in school when I was the sports editor for our weekly high school paper, and I thoroughly enjoyed writing about the sports accomplishments of my friends. As soon as I retired, I began taking writing classes and received encouragement from the instructor. I wrote the first 30 chapters of my first book, *My 36 Years in Space*, but set it aside when I realized that publishing a book required more knowledge in the field. Seventeen years later, I finally published it. I was saddened and embarrassed to realize I could have completed it while my mother and sister were still alive. Eventually, I researched the publishing field and overcame major obstacles by self-publishing. While I continue to enjoy the writing; the editing, publishing, marketing, and distribution remain challenges.

Gambling

In 1970 we experienced our first casino in Las Vegas, the Hacienda (now replaced by Mandalay Bay). After flying from Houston and taking the taxi, we arrived at 10 PM. Sue immediately sat down at an all-jackpot five-cent slot machine just inside the Hacienda door and started playing. I checked in, took the luggage to our room, and joined her at the adjacent machine. I was losing and she was winning when I decided to call it a night; she said she would be right up. The next morning, I awoke at 8 AM and came down to find her still at the same machine. Her tray was full of nickels, her arms were black from handling the coins, and she was pulling the lever with her left hand because her right arm was so tired and aching. Being new to gambling, I tried every game they offered until we went home two days later with minor losses. It was great entertainment.

But after we returned home, I read books on gambling and learned that most slots were set so that the house returned only 83-88% of the money fed into them. The odds are better for the high value machines of $1 and $5 slots. These odds are often printed on the equipment. The worst table game for the player is the Wheel of Fortune also called the Big Six Wheel. The $1 segment has the lowest edge for the house at 11%. The odds get worse as the segment goes up with the $20 and the Joker segments having a 24% edge for the house. Roulette is also not a great choice if you want to win over the long haul, unless you stick to the bets of *Red* and *Black* or *Odd* and *Even* at 5 % in favor of the casino. Craps are only 1.4% in favor of the house if you stick to the *Pass* and *Don't Pass* lines or *Come* and *Don't Come* lines. But betting on the higher payout lines, like the *Field* are more heavily in favor of the house. However, if you bet "the Odds" that the shooter will make his point, the house has no edge at all.

My favorite is Blackjack. If you follow the basic strategy documented in any Blackjack book, the house has less than 1% in its favor. And if you "count" accurately, you can even get odds slightly in your favor, which is why the casino is on the lookout for "counters" and will ban them if they catch them, even though it is not illegal to count. With enough practice, it is possible to learn counting. I learned how to count and usually win a little at Blackjack. But I make sure to concentrate intently and avoid alcohol when playing Blackjack. Some people say such intense concentration reduces the fun of gambling. But I enjoy winning money, while others at my table are losing. I try to play at the cheaper $5 tables because I do not want to attract attention by counting, which might attract more attention at $10 and $15 tables.

I learned never to play Blackjack without refreshing my mind with the Basic Strategy.

Hypnosis

As a teen in the mid-1950's, I was interested in some unusual phenomena. One of the most fascinating was hypnosis. Could someone really exercise control of someone else's mind beyond what the individual himself desired? Can the mind control physical bodily functions, otherwise thought to be uncontrollable?

I began reading about the subject, from clinical books on hypnosis to stage entertainment where a "hypnotist" would hypnotize people out of the audience to do things for the amusement of the rest of the crowd. I learned that many of the wives' tales were untrue. Hypnosis is NOT the phenomenon of stronger minds dominating weaker minds. In fact, people of low intelligence generally make poor subjects, while many with sharp minds make good subjects. This is because concentration is a key factor to being a good subject. One class of intelligent people who do not make good subjects are those who tend to over-analyze what the hypnotist is saying, thus losing the intense focus on his words. While most people can be hypnotized to some extent, only 20% can enter a deep, somnambulistic state, and then only with the help of a skilled hypnotist. Nevertheless, beneficial medical treatments, such as pain relief, insomnia, overeating, incontinence in children, and physical problems with a psychological component, such as circulatory problems, are evident even in lighter states.

I read about the history of hypnosis, including the first "hypnotist." The 18th century German physician, Franz Mesmer, induced various patients into a hypnotic state to control their physical ailments and published the results in 1775. As a demonstration of the power, he was reputed to have hypnotized subjects into such a deep sleep that their blood stopped flowing, their pulses stopped, their breathing ceased, and they were pronounced dead by other physicians of that era. Then he supposedly brought them back to life by simply awakening them from this "trance." This is where the term "mesmerism" was derived to describe someone in this deep sleep or trance. I continued to devour everything that I could lay may hands on about the subject: books, magazine articles, newspaper articles. It was fascinating to me. But, as a teen, I never tried it.

It is not necessarily true that "one cannot cause a subject to do something he would not want to do." Generally, if the hypnotist is trusted, a good subject wants to do whatever the hypnotist says. This is partially because the hypnotist has induced the feeling similar to falling asleep, an extremely comfortable and pleasurable state. The subject is grateful to the person who induced this pleasure and wants to please in return, thereby tending to follow the hypnotist's instruction if he can. The subject is intensely focused on the hypnotist's voice and instructions, shutting out the rest of the world, and thereby better able to carry out the instructions.

In 1952, an amateur hypnotist, Morey Bernstein, used hypnotic regression to take a young housewife in Pueblo, Colorado into the 'life before her life." That is, while in a deep state, he took her backward in her life year-by-year until he told her that she was in a life prior to the one in which she now lived (i.e., reincarnation). He told her to tell him details of this life, which she did over a series of many hypnotic sessions. She said her name was Bridey Murphy, living in 19th century Ireland, and said it often with an Irish brogue. She even sang Irish songs. Bernstein published the results of his many sessions with the housewife in a 1956 best-selling book, *The Search for Bridey Murphy*. This led many at the time to begin to believe in reincarnation. The Broadway play, *On a Clear Day (You Can See Forever)*, about the Bridey Murphy tale was a hit in 1965, and the movie of the same name was also popular in 1970. However, the credibility of the Bridey Murphy story was repudiated when a reporter discovered the housewife grew up across the street from a Bridey Murphy, who shared tales of Ireland, and the housewife learned the Irish brogue and Irish jigs as a schoolgirl. It was not that she was lying, but rather that when asked to recall, she used both her recollection of her childhood and her imagination to tell the hypnotist what he apparently wanted to hear. This was very consistent with subjects who are asked to respond to questions they cannot immediately answer. They dig into their pasts and their imaginations to give the hypnotist "proper" answers, now known as false memories. One of my favorite films, *Manchurian Candidate* (1962) goes a step farther to use brain washing and post hypnotic suggestions to amplify on the power of hypnosis. The novel, *False Memory*, by Dean Koontz puts them all together.

In my first real job at the age of 15, selling magazines door-to-door, I had my first direct experience with the real process of hypnosis. One of the guys in our crew was a hypnotist. At age 17, he had been practicing it for two years. As we rode in the station wagon to our territory of the day, he told me about his first-hand experiences. He claimed to be proficient at putting subjects "under." He had done it many times. But he also cautioned that it was critical that the hypnotist knew what he was doing; otherwise it could be dangerous.

One day, he demonstrated the proper technique on the way to the territory. Another 15-year-old wanted to quit smoking but had not been successful. We watched as he "put him under," successively telling him to go into a deeper and deeper sleep, testing his susceptibility to the suggestions as he progressed. He was an excellent subject. When he reached the proper depth, the hypnotist gave him a cigarette and told him to light up. But first, he told him it would taste like seaweed every time he took a drag. The subject then lit up, made a terrible face, and spit out the cigarette with disgust. The hypnotist then slowly brought him back to reality. But it worked. The subject quit smoking because of the terrible taste. The hypnotist later explained why he had caused the subject to quit on his own volition, rather than giving him the command never to smoke again. The subject would otherwise be frustrated, not understanding why he "couldn't" smoke even though he enjoyed it and wanted to smoke. This unknown frustration could lead to neuroses or even psychoses.

He later demonstrated the entertainment value of hypnosis for us by doing age regression on a 20-year-old college student, a big football player type. He took him back to age three and had him reciting baby talk, which was a riot.

The 17-year-old also explained that he was able to hypnotize himself into a light state prior to studying. Thus, he could concentrate intently on his study material, even memorizing it verbatim. At test time, he could totally recall the relevant page of the text and "see" the words on the page. He explained that if he went beyond the light state, it would not work because he would truly fall asleep and be unable to "instruct himself" to study.

I tried self-hypnosis before studying, but without any success. The only times I noticed any real help was when I had trouble falling asleep. I would lay flat on the bed, arms and legs outstretched, and would begin by telling myself "toes, fall asleep," then "metatarsals, fall asleep," continuing upward sequentially for all the parts of my body. Usually, by the time I reached my midsection, I was asleep.

But in graduate school at the University of Wisconsin in 1963, I had a hypnosis "encounter of the third kind." I was successful in applying for an assignment as a residence counselor in a male dormitory. In return for room, board, and tuition, I was responsible for the academic, physical, and behavioral well-being of 30 undergraduate boys, the vast majority of whom were freshmen. One day after dinner, I started telling some of them about hypnosis. They were fascinated. Before I knew it, nearly the whole dorm was in my office, adjacent to my bedroom, listening to my dissertation about the subject. Naturally, they asked whether I had ever hypnotized anyone. Of course, when I said I had not, they dared me to do it.

A freshman from Boston, Mark Lipton, volunteered to be the subject. I had to try it to save face. I called on all the techniques I had learned. I sat Mark in a comfortable chair and told him to concentrate on my voice and watch my finger intently as I slowly moved it from left to right and back, over, and over. I told him he was becoming so tired. His eyelids were becoming so heavy he could not keep them open. His eyes eventually closed.

"Try to open your eyes, Mark. You cannot. Your lids are too heavy." Mark turned out to be an excellent subject. For each command he obeyed, he became more and more trusting in my instructions.

"You may stop trying to open them. You are falling into a deeper and deeper sleep. Relax all your muscles. You are feeling very relaxed and comfortable. You are enjoying this feeling and the sound of my voice. You can only hear my voice, nothing else." This was necessary for him not to become distracted by the giggling and murmuring of the 20+ kids watching all this.

Next, I tested him to see if he was susceptible to a more difficult suggestion. Normally this would happen in a second session, but I had not intended for this to become repeat performances.

"Mark, I want you to extend your right arm. It is becoming very rigid, like an iron rod. You cannot begin to bend it; it is so rigid. Try, Mark; try to bend it. You cannot." Indeed, he could not, as his fist was turning white and his extended arm was shaking.

"Okay Mark. You can now relax your arm and can bend it. It has returned to normal. Let it sit in your lap. You are now going into a deeper sleep, feeling wonderful. Deeper, deeper." This demonstrated he was indeed susceptible and an excellent subject.

"Now, Mark, I am going to take you back in your life to your early years. You are 17 years old. We will count backward as you go back in your life. You are now 16; now 15, 14, 13, 12, 11. Where are you, Mark?" He answered he was in 6th grade.

"Who is your teacher? Who is sitting at your right?" He answered easily.

"Now we are going back farther. You are now 9; now 8. Who is your teacher, Mark? How many windows are in the room? Who is sitting to your right?" He was unable to answer the last two questions.

"When I count three, you will be able to answer." I repeated each question, and after each I counted "one, two, three." On the count of three each time, he gave me an answer.

"Mark, we are now going back farther…7…6…. You are now six years old. Where are you? Who is your teacher? Who sits in front of you? Who sits behind?" Again, I had to use the technique of his being able to answer when I counted three, which appeared to work, since he was again able to answer.

"Mark, after you awaken, I want you to do something for me. Every time I ask you who your favorite baseball player is, you will answer *Eddie Mathews*." (Mathews was MY favorite baseball player, an all-star third baseman who played for the Milwaukee Braves from the time they moved from Boston in 1953 to the present 1963.)

"Now Mark, I will count to ten. On the count of ten, you will wake up, totally refreshed and feeling good." On the count of ten, he awoke to the applause of the 20+ kids, felt fine, but his right arm ached, and he looked a little confused.

"When are we going to start? Weren't you able to hypnotize me?" I explained to him all that had transpired, except the Eddie Mathews post-hypnotic suggestion.

"Mark, do you remember your 6th grade teacher?" He answered all the questions the same way he did under hypnosis, except the ones I had to empower him to answer. These he could not remember. When I gave him some of the answers, he was surprised and confirmed them. But some answers he did not even recognize when I told him what he had stated under the hypnosis enabler. Sporadically during all this post hypnotic questioning, I popped in with "By the way, who's your favorite baseball player?"

He immediately smiled and said, "Eddie Mathews!" The guys roared with laughter.

Once, I followed up with, "What position does he play?"

He looked quizzical and slowly answered, "Left Field?" Laughter.

Later, "What team does he play for?"

Again, slowly, and quizzically, "Boston Red Sox?" More laughter. Mark looked bewildered.

I finally explain to him that this was a post hypnotic suggestion. But he emphatically **insisted** Eddie Mathews **is** his favorite baseball player. It took me a long time to convince him that this was only due to hypnosis. (I am not sure he is convinced to this day.) He was clearly disturbed by this contradiction in his mind. I never tried hypnosis again. Today, Mark is a practicing psychologist and uses hypnosis in his practice in Madison, Wisconsin.

9. AMERICAN POLITICS

I tackle this subject with some trepidation because it is emotionally seated with many people. We do not want to hear advice that differs from our deep-seated convictions. To be honest, I am afraid I too fall into this category. But the book would not be complete without including politics in America.

I began my adult life as a social moderate, maybe a liberal, but a fiscal conservative. However, after implementing Affirmative Action Plans for decades and witnessing unsuccessful social programs to help the poor and minorities, instead of helping people to be self-reliant, I concluded these programs are perpetuating the social status of those we are trying to help. They solidify generation after generation of dependency. There are exceptions, of course, but if we treat people as a downtrodden class, this class will remain downtrodden. One of my favorite quotes comes from Henry Ford, "Whether you think you can, or you think you can't—you're right."

I have come to believe that the intent of many liberal politicians is to keep us dependent on the government so we are beholden to the politicians, thus enhancing their reelection prospects and enabling them to retain power over the people.

When I was young, I used to respect most congressmen. Now that I have become cynical, I dislike most politicians; to me they put their own selfish desire for power and re-election ahead of what is best for their constituents. Unfortunately, corruption is evident. How many career politicians, never working in the private sector have used their power in high office to enrich themselves, their families, and their friends? They are now multi-millionaires with several expensive homes. The most obvious example of this lies in the Clinton Foundation. Peter Schweizer recently released a best seller, *Profiles in Corruption,* describing these horrible actions by our political "leaders." Power corrupts and absolute power corrupts absolutely. Strict term limits might help.

I believe all governments have this failing. But I do believe our system of government is better than any other, unfortunately. However, this power drug motivates our politicians to enact more laws and regulations that get in the way of free enterprise, both for companies and individuals, while enriching themselves. Oh, I agree that some of these regulations and laws are valuable, even necessary. But if the authors of the Constitution and the Bill of Rights saw what this country must deal with today, I am convinced they would be appalled.

I personally had to deal with thousands of pages of Federal Regulations for acquisition of military and NASA products and services throughout most of my career. These regulations alone are the causes of the $48 hammer and the $640 toilet seat, because the profit margin for the companies that charge these prices is less than 10%.

Our government at every level is bloated. Civil servants' salaries are heavily weighted for how many people one manages. So, if one can get away with more people to accomplish a task (and adhere to all the regulations), he/she is motivated to do so. And it is considered unsatisfactory if the public sector manager does not spend all his budget every fiscal year, because otherwise it would be difficult to justify the next year's bloated increase. Exactly the opposite is true in private business where competition drives efficiency. Therefore, it is not surprising that the private sector does a job better than a government enterprise.

Perhaps the most obvious relationship between the civil servants and politicians occurs at the state and local levels, to the detriment of the taxpayer. At one time, the civil servant's salary was lower than a counterpart in private industry. The bureaucracy and its unions used this difference to extract better benefits, particularly paid absences, holidays, heath care, and, most of all, retirement benefits. The civil servant unions continued to extract concessions from the local governments by donating to reelection campaigns. In turn the politicians granted big benefits. So today we have professors, firemen, policemen, and others earning large salaries, retiring at age 50 or 55, and receiving lifetime pensions and medical insurance that the cities, counties, and states cannot afford and are unsustainable. When they run out of taxpayer money, it is not clear how the municipal and state bankruptcies will shake out.

It does not get any better on the national level. Our congress has created a national debt of more than $26,300,000,000,000. That amounts to $80,000 for every single person in America. And today it would seem that no politician has the courage to address the problem. It will only get worse. This will not end well. If interest rates return to normal, we will have to default on the debt.

I anticipate that my opinions on this subject are controversial; I do not expect to change anyone's mind today. But eventually we voters will have to solve these problems.

10. INVESTMENTS– DO IT YOURSELF

In my opinion investing should be a mandatory course in college. Of course, it was years after we were married that I even had enough money to invest, so maybe I would have forgotten much of what I learned in class. But I still think it would have saved me from making some mistakes. It is good advice to save enough liquid assets (rainy day fund) to live on for six months before beginning to invest. Even tenured teachers can be laid off, and it could take six months to find a comparable job in a recession.

Expert Advice?

My first plunge into the market was the $7,000 we made on selling our first home in 1967. I contacted Merrill Lynch and met a young broker/advisor. After several discussions, I agreed to invest in a stock in which all seven research analysts gave a *buy* recommendation. When the stocked dropped in value and the analysts still recommended *buy,* I invested more of my stash. How could all seven be wrong? Well, they were wrong, and I lost a big chunk of my money. After I sold, it kept going down before the analysts finally changed their recommendations to *hold* and then *sell*. I wish the wise bird could have told me that analysts can be incompetent.

So, maybe the best way to invest in equities is to leave it to the professional managers of mutual funds. After all, they do this full time and have many credentials that validate their knowledge and competence, right? Also, they must have a good performance track record or investors would not give them their money. Wrong on both counts! According to *Payback Time* by Phil Town, only three (0.05%) of all mutual funds have consistently beaten the averages over the past 15 years. Of course, we do not learn this from the investment community. They continue to advertise the big lie: that only the professionals know how to pick stocks; individual investors do not stand a chance. It is true that they cannot have a poor performance record to stay in business, but they simply close their poorly performing fund and start a new one, so their poor record is "expunged."

Could I do better myself?

With a little work and a lot of discipline, the individual investor should beat the big guys consistently. First, the individual can buy and sell without affecting the price of the stock. When the big mutual funds buy, they must do it over some length of time because the large orders drive the price up while they are buying. Therefore, their average purchase price is higher that the individual's low-volume single trade. Similarly, when they sell, they have the same problem, driving the price down, and selling at a lower average price than the individual's single transaction. Next, the big funds cannot buy just a few companies' stocks. The

Securities and Exchange Commission's regulations typically require that they limit their holdings in a single company to 5% of the total value of all their holdings. Other rules cause the biggest funds to own stocks in dozens, perhaps hundreds of companies to spread their risk. So instead of putting all their money in a few superstar companies, they are forced to buy many that they may not really want to own. The individual, of course, has no such constraint.

The biggest reason the individual can do better is by avoiding the fees they charge for managing your money. When you add up the fees they charge to pay their salaries, commissions, overhead, administration, and profit for the firm, the fees total as much as 2% of the value your investment for every year in which they manage your money. So, if in a good year, your investment went up 10%, they take 2%, leaving you 8% (taking 20% of your gain). But in a bad year, if your holdings tanked 10%, you actually lose 12%, because they still keep their 2%. These may not seem like big numbers in a single year, but compounded over a lifetime of investing, they can rob you of approximately 60% of the gains you would have made if these fees were zero. And guess what? They got rich on your money, while you barely kept up with inflation. Even if you were lucky enough to never lose money, and the market went up 8% every year, their fees rob you. If you invested $10,000 per year for 35 years at 8% return each year with no fees, you would have over $2 million. But if they took their 2% each year, you would have $1.27 million. And if you continued this investment for 60 years without fees, you would be worth over $13.5 million, compared to $5.66 million when they take their annual 2%. Today, most mutual fund managers have reduced their fees to 1% because the individual investor is demanding it. The lesson for me is not to pay money managers to manage your portfolio unless you do not have the discipline to manage it yourself.

But can we really avoid these fees? Well, we can avoid at least 90% of them. If we buy individual stocks on our own (rather than asking the broker to place the trades) using an online discount brokerage, the only fees we pay are brokerage transaction fees, which today are zero for most discount brokerage accounts. Buying and selling individual companies' stock requires some real effort to determine the best buys and when to sell, but it can be done. After reading several books, I did it successfully for a few years, beating the market averages. The strategy that worked well for me was based on technical charting. I selected 70 value stocks (those in which their intrinsic value was above the current price) and tracked them daily to build Point and Figure Charts, then used these charts to determine *buy* and *sell* signals. At any one time I never owned more than a dozen of the stocks I was tracking. The problem was I was spending 1-2 hours every day to keep up. There are many other technical strategies using charts.

Stock picking is not easy. It is said that a monkey throwing darts at a listing of all 3500 publicly traded US stocks does as well as the experts. This would seem to promote investing in the broad indices of stocks, such as the S&P 500, the 30 Dow Jones Industrials, the Nasdaq, and the FTSE, by buying Exchange Traded Funds (ETF)s of these indices.

For several years, I simply bought ETFs, diversified across loosely correlated categories of stocks and bonds, then rebalanced periodically. I spent less than one hour per month once I set up the system. Why ETFs? These are funds that are not actively managed, but rather just track indices of broad stock and bond categories. For example, one can buy ETF shares of the S&P 500 index (e.g., SPY, VOO, VXX), which tracks the weighted average of the 500 largest companies in the United States. So, this investment goes up and down almost exactly with all the stocks of the 500 companies. Every year, more than 90% of the mutual funds do not beat the performance of the S&P 500, net of fees. And what are the annual fees that the ETF takes out of your investment? As low as 0.03%. So, on an investment of $10,000, it costs you $3 per year. Quite a difference from the mutual fund managers' annual fee of at least $100.

To give another quantified example on the cost of paying management fees: Say you hired a money manager and gave him $100 each month to invest for you. He invests your money in the S&P 500 index that returned 8% per year, and he charged you a 1% fee (expense ratio) for this service. As an alternative, instead you invested directly (through your online broker) in the Vanguard S&P 500 index fund VOO, earning the same 8% per year. with a 0.03% expense ratio. After 30 years, you would have earned $21,841 more doing it yourself. Another example illustrates the dramatic difference of beginning to save and invest at an early age. If you began investing $100 per month at age 21 and earned 8% annually, you would have $524,000 for retirement at age 65. But, if you waited until age 30 to start investing, you would only have $254,000 at age 65.

Portfolio Allocation

Then there is the issue of portfolio allocation. What percent of your money should be in stocks vs. bonds? Asset allocation can be a complex subject. But it can lower the risk of portfolio losses easier than trying to time the market. Without delving into the complexities of Modern Portfolio Theory, I will highlight some of the issues and some conclusions. The objective of portfolio allocation is to reduce overall risk by dividing your savings between asset classes that do not closely correlate. Diversity is the issue here. A diversified portfolio would begin with allocations between equities (stocks) and fixed income (e.g., bonds) because these are two primary classes not closely correlated. Ostensibly, when one asset class decreases in value, the other increases.

Stock equities appreciate the most over the long term, but also incur the higher risk of losing value. Bonds generally are lower risk but appreciate less, usually only by paying the interest. But bonds do have two kinds of risk: 1) default wherein the entity issuing the bonds goes bankrupt and cannot pay back the debt, and 2) increases in prevailing interest rates, causing the bond with its fixed rate to go down in value. (But if current interest rates go down, the bond's value should increase.) The lowest risk bonds, US government treasuries, also pay the lowest interest rate. Today these interest rates are so low that they should be avoided. Long term bonds pay higher rates but have more interest rate risk. Corporate bonds pay higher rates according to their risk of default and are given risk ratings accordingly, from highest grade (AAA) to lowest investment grade (BBB), down to junk bonds (lower than BBB). So, if the stock market takes a big hit, the value of the bonds in your portfolio are supposed to increase, but by a lower percentage.

The higher the allocation of stocks to bonds, the higher expected return over the long term, coupled with the inherent risk. The higher allocation of bonds to stocks, the lower risk, but lower expected return. Most recommend a high, aggressive allocation to stocks (say 80%) if you are investing for the long term (e. g., greater than 10 years), but if you are concerned about the short term (less than five years), you may want to reduce the risk by allocating as much as 80% to bonds, only 20% to stocks. Years ago, before the Federal Reserve reduced the federal funds rate to zero, sage advice said to allocate 60% to stocks and 40% to bonds. This was a cornerstone for decades. But with treasury bonds so low today, this would result in a poor rate of return for our portfolio.

With taking on more risk, our fixed income allocation works better with corporate bonds or preferred stock.

Inflation should also be considered, which is another reason to prefer stocks to bonds. So, at age 79 years, I thought I was being conservative to protect our retirement nest egg by a heavy allocation to short term corporate bonds over stocks. I was quite surprised when my bonds decreased in value by 10% while my stocks plunged 30% during the first month of the Covid-19 pandemic. My bonds took the hit along with the stocks because their risk of default dramatically increased as the economy was shutting down. Of course, if the company issuing the bonds were in such trouble that they went out of business, truly defaulting and declaring bankruptcy, then both their stock and their bonds could go to zero. In practice, even if they did declare bankruptcy and their stock became worthless, their corporate assets would be liquidated to pay off the bond holders, but likely at less than full value.

In turn, you can diversify within a class. One example of diversification of US equities has been a mainstay of the investment strategy of a friend of mine. He allocates 60% of his portfolio to a Large Capitalization ETF, 15% to a Mid Cap ETF, and 25% to a Small Cap ETF with a buy-and-hold bent. This has done well for him during the bull market this past decade. But there are many more portfolio allocation possibilities: real estate (land and buildings), precious metals (gold and silver), and other diversification subsets of both stocks and bonds. A key issue is the degree of correlation between these assets. The less correlation, the more diversity, and therefore less total risk. The best diversification with no market correlation is gold, which is why gold usually increases in value when the economy is in trouble or when inflation is high. At one point I invested a small portion of my portfolio in gold to diversify my portfolio. I bought the gold ETF IAU, so I would not have to mess with the sales, storage fees, and insurance with the hard metal. I made a small gain, but then sold it, when I realized there is no gain (e.g., dividends or interest) if the gold price remained flat. Later, I did buy a gold mining ETF, GDX, that paid a small dividend.

This is how I diversified my investments between the two major asset classes (equities and fixed income) to reduce risk. I first used the guideline of investing in equities (stocks) with a fixed percentage of my portfolio. This percentage is determined by age as: 120 minus one's age. So, at age 50, I invest 70% in equities and 30% in fixed income (e.g., bonds, certificates of deposit, bank savings accounts, and cash). At age 70, I invest 50% in equities, leaving 50% in fixed income. This formula shows you can take more risk by having a larger portion of your portfolio in stocks because you have time to recoup if you take a big hit in the market. But even when you are older, it is important to have a significant percentage in the equity market to deal with inflation. One can break the equities down into categories such as Large Cap (big companies), Mid Cap, Small Cap, growth, value, utilities, real estate, commodities (e.g., precious metals, oil, gas), private companies in developed foreign countries (e.g., Germany, France, Canada, Australia), and emerging markets (e.g., China, India, Brazil). Other diversified alternatives include the eleven sectors of the market. The fixed-income class includes such categories as short, medium, and long-term treasuries, Treasury Inflation-Protected Securities (TIPS), corporate bonds, high yield (junk) bonds, preferred stocks, and cash (e.g., money markets, certificates of deposit, bank savings accounts).

You can allocate a fixed percentage of your savings to each category or subset, then rebalance back to the original allocation percentage whenever any of them deviates significantly from their initial respective percentages. Some investors rebalance annually or quarterly. By spreading savings across loosely correlated categories, one reduces the impact of major losses to the total portfolio when one or more categories have losses. Rebalancing can result in beating the averages since you sell high (when the category has done much better than the others) and buy low (when one category has done poorly compared to the others). Historically each category above has been both a best performer some years and worst performer in other years. We cannot predict which will do best, so we rebalance instead. Over the past decade of a record bull market, 100% equities has obviously performed best.

While I was working, I invested most of my money over the years in my 401(k). Because I was a long way from retirement, I chose to go with 100% equities, which worked well even through the stock market swings. (If I did it over, based on the advice of the wise bird, I would have allocated at least 15% to fixed income.) But I realized that these 401(k) funds were extracting more than a 1% fee from my account, which clearly came out of my portfolio each month whether the fund made money or lost it.

Market Timing

The two human emotions of fear and greed can play a strong role in investing. It is easy to tell yourself that you have the discipline to ignore your emotions, and always use logic for your investment decisions, but it is exceedingly difficult to do so. At least it was for me. When the coronavirus hit, dropping the stock markets over 30% in a month, I sold some of my holdings, only to watch them climb, then wildly swing. It is so tempting to let fear take over and sell low as your stocks are plummeting and then rebuy high when the market is souring. How far do you let it go down before selling? What do you do with the cash? When is the right time to get back in? And when you do, what do you do when it plummets again? This is market timing, which the experts say cannot be done. This explains why Warren Buffet's strategy has been "buy and hold." But his strategy has been under attack in recent years.

As mentioned earlier, there are eleven sectors which comprise the total US equity market, such as health care, financials, information technology, real estate, energy, industrials, etc. If you believe a particular sector is underpriced, based on forecasting the future, you can invest in an index that tracks that sector. But you may be wrong about the sector being undervalued. And even if you are right, when do you sell? Or buy more when that sector goes down in value?

The experts say it is impossible to time the market; that is to buy low and sell high. Basically, that is true; no one is smart enough to know when to get in and get out. If we KNEW exactly how to time market ups and downs, we could make a fortune. Still, it is possible to spot a "bubble." When I retired in 1999 from TRW, I elected to take my pension in a lump sum, rather than monthly checks because the payments would not go up with inflation, and Sue would get nothing if I died first. I added it to the IRA which I converted from the 401(k). I could now control the investments for the IRA and avoid the 1% annual mutual fund management fee.

But now the question became how to invest the lump sum. If I wanted to duplicate the constant monthly distributions TRW offered, I could have bought an annuity. But I thought I could do better. In 1999 and early 2000, all the equity markets were appreciating dramatically, especially the Internet market segment (Dotcom's). But no one knew when the correction would happen. If I got out a year early before the peak, I could miss stocks doubling or even more.

So, I decided to invest in hedge funds. I engaged a broker from one of the traditional investment houses, A.G. Edwards, a full-service securities broker-dealer. I really did not know how to check out his reputation, other than asking about his track record. He suggested some hedge funds to address my concern about the risk of the market being overheated. After studying some marketing material from the two funds he had recommended, and paying special attention to their past performance, I invested $100,000 in each. These were two funds that stated their strategy was to invest approximately 67% "long" (buying stocks they believed would go up) and 33% "short" (borrowing stocks and selling them with the promise to pay them back after they had fallen in value). I thought this would be a good hedge against the major correction coming sometime in the future. I did my due diligence on the ones recommended by the broker (which he claimed he invested for his retired parents), being impressed with the track record these hedge firms had in the past. Well, it turned out that I was right about the market because the bubble burst and it took a nose drive. The Nasdaq market dropped 77% from its high in 19 months. One fund worked well: while the total market dropped more than 50% in 2000-2002, my investment value stayed flat. The other hedge fund, however lost 50% right with the market, because the idiot NEVER sold a single stock short! When I called my broker to sell, I learned he had left the financial services business. I probably should have tried to get AG Edwards to reimburse me for the fraudulent statement that the hedge fund did not follow through on their stated strategy, but that might have involved litigation, which meant attorney fees. I clearly needed an advisor at this point. The lesson learned was to do my own investing instead of hiring an "expert."

If you are saving monthly and regularly investing, a technique that works well to avoid trying to time the market is Dollar Cost Averaging. This means that if you invest a fixed amount each month, you do well over the long haul because when the ETF is down you are buying more shares than when the ETF is up.

Income Tax Suggestions

Income tax on investments will play a role in your portfolio growth. But this should not affect your decisions on whether to avoid selling a stock just to avoid the federal income tax on the gains. If you believe that you should sell because the stock is overbought and the price is too high, do not hesitate to sell. One possible exception is long-term capital gains. If you hold a stock for at least 365 days and sell at a profit, the federal capital gains tax will likely be lower than the ordinary income tax. Some states, like California, do not recognize long-term capital gains. They tax all such gains as ordinary income.

You can avoid income tax on both federal and state by creating a Roth account and funding it with earned income. You must pay ordinary income tax initially on the income, but from that point on the Roth can grow indefinitely without paying income tax on the gains. A Roth strategy can work well in your early adult life when your income tax bracket is low. The Roth funds should be invested in growth stocks because you plan to hold it for decades.

Funding a 401(k) or IRA is a compromise on tax deferral. You will defer income tax on any earned income with which you fund the IRA until you make an IRA withdrawal. At that time, you must pay tax on the withdrawal at ordinary income tax rates. Unfortunately, if the withdrawal is later in life you may be in a higher income tax bracket than when you funded the IRA. The big advantage is that your IRA nest egg can grow and compound untaxed for decades before you elect to take withdrawals.

However, when you reach age 70.5 you are required to begin withdrawals each year, based on an age-dependent formula.

My advice is not to withdraw from your IRA until it is necessary, ideally after age 70.5. Spend from your investments outside the IRA and Roth first. When those investments are exhausted, start withdrawing and spending the IRA assets. Lastly, only after the IRA is exhausted, start withdrawing and spending the Roth.

Of course, the federal and state tax laws are subject to change, based on the infinite wisdom of our politicians. These changes could affect the plans described above. It is valuable to understand the provisos of both the state and federal tax codes. You can get a solid understanding by doing your own income tax returns. If you could find a competent professional to do so, hire him/her to only review your completed returns to see if you missed anything.

I have used both *Turbo Tax* and *Tax Act* software to complete my returns but discovered they too can make an error, but rarely. I now believe I am income tax proficient. I have never experienced an audit. But I learned that calling the IRS to get questions answered was a waste of time. It takes time to reach help via phone. But also, they can give wrong answers. You are responsible for the accuracy of the returns, no matter who advises you. If you hire a professional to do them, make sure you understand every step he/she executes. I tried four different Certified Public Accountants over the 60 years to generate and file my returns. Each time I found significant errors, some in my favor, others not. Of course, I never engaged any of these CPAs again. They were not incompetent, but rather they were careless.

If leaving a monetary legacy to your heirs is important, be aware that when you die, both your home and your portfolio is stepped up in value at the time of your death and the gains realized up to that point are not taxed. (Of course, that is also true of your Roth assets.) But your IRA bequeathed to your heirs will require income tax over a period of time which they have options to declare. It is valuable to your heirs to avoid probate when you die. Most set up a trust to avoid probate, but a lawyer may not be required, although highly recommended for safety. You may be able to use legal software to set up the trust, provided you fund it properly.

Alternative Investments

I have tried other alternative investments over the years, but in most cases, I would not recommend them. In the early 1980's I invested in two limited partnerships in large apartment complexes. I lost money in both, primarily because the timing in real estate was not good. The peak had been reached in the 1979-80 timeframe and headed south for several years. I thought I had done my due diligence into the track records of the general partners, but that was not enough. The timing was critical.

In the late 1980's I hired a Certified Public Accountant to file my income tax returns. My income was high due to my annual bonus earned as a general manager at Intermetrics, and the CPA told me I needed a tax shelter. He suggested the oil drilling company in which he had invested his mother's savings. I did check with some current investors in the projects, but they were not sophisticated enough to give me much insight. I ended up investing $30,000 that I wrote off in three years. But when the price of oil dropped to $17 per barrel the revenue was insufficient to pay for the leases, the drilling, and the operations. The company folded and our leases were worthless. The CPA was a con man, was arrested by the FBI several years later, and was serving time at the age of 70. Lesson: Do not invest in something you know nothing about with people you do not know. Sure, if the leases were active a few years ago, we could have made big money with oil at $100 per barrel, but this was more than a timing issue. Where was the wise bird when I needed him most?

In the 90's when real estate in Southern California had bottomed out, I wanted to invest in it. I met a man named John Trainer, who had been mentored by a successful, wealthy, real estate investor. After a few meetings with Trainer, it was clear he was intelligent, hardworking, and had acquired some good ideas on how to find undervalued, small apartment complexes in the Los Angeles area. Trainer formed a limited partnership to buy a six-unit apartment in Hawthorne, California. He gave me a full presentation on his business plan with pictures of the building. His plan was to buy the building for an attractive price, then improve it before finding renters. He planned to raise $165,000 to cover the down payment, the renovation expenses, and sufficient capital to cover operating losses until it was fully rented. I bought in for $20,000, giving me a 12.12% stake. Over the next five years, I ended up investing in ten different Trainer Limited Partnerships for apartment complexes that were never larger than 16 units. Trainer did a great job in finding distressed sales, evaluating dozens of properties for each one he bought.

At first these investments were performing very well. Not only was their value appreciating, but I was getting $15,000 per year in distributed net profits from the rental operations. But suddenly Trainer was no longer keeping up with the quarterly and annual reporting. When the payments fell off, I personally did an audit on the investments. Trainer was out of the office when I showed up to quiz him on the operations. His small staff let me examine the cancelled checks involving the rental operations. I discovered enough to prove he was embezzling most of the net proceeds and co-mingling funds. Although this might be enough to get law enforcement into the picture, I realized it would not be a priority for them. Instead I tried to pressure Trainer into distributing our profits. But I was stonewalled. The only way to get our operating income was to hire an attorney and have Trainer and his accountant removed. As general partner, he had total authority in all decisions. I also dealt with his unethical CPA. I clearly needed some sound advice as to how to deal with this crook. I did talk to an attorney, but his fee would have wiped out my original investment. (John realized this and made sure that he always had at least six limited partners and did his best to not let any of us learn the names and phone numbers of the others.) And had we won in court; I would be faced with the task of managing the property. Even so, when we finally sold the last of properties, I had doubled my initial investments, validating my instincts and timing.

    The last of these properties went into foreclosure for the property taxes Trainer had not paid. I ultimately recovered $80,000 for my $35,000 investment (initiated more than twelve years earlier), but John embezzled an equal amount of my share as well as that owned by the other investors. Trainer stiffed his investors on other properties in which I was not involved, fled to Texas, and was a fugitive from the law. I do not know whether he was brought to justice. We would have made much more money had he not neglected the properties and paid the mortgage and taxes on time. Some were seized by the mortgage holder or the state for lack of payment and sold at auction. The lesson? Limited partners do not have control. We rely entirely on the competence and honesty of the general partner. Real estate investing can be lucrative with the right timing and locations, but lack of control can sour any deal, especially if the general partner becomes corrupt.

Annuities

Annuities are insurance products usually used to guarantee or supplement income during retirement. They come in a variety of complexities and options.

At one time, I considered buying an annuity to ensure we had enough guaranteed income from it to live comfortably the rest of our lives. Some "experts" tell me this is the worst way to invest for several reasons: the fees are too high; the payments are fixed, not increasing with inflation; the contracts lock in for several years with a penalty for early withdrawal; you leave nothing as a legacy when you die; if you want your spouse to continue to receive the payments when you die, you have to accept a lower payment. But, if the market drops significantly as it did due to the 2020 economy shutdown caused by the coronavirus, your contract remains safe, unless the issuing insurance company goes bankrupt. Nevertheless, in 2017 when I thought the market was overbought, I did invest my Roth IRA money (7% of my total portfolio) in a nine-year annuity, which can go up, but not down. This annuity has minimal fees and if I withdraw a maximum of 10% annually, I incur no penalties. Although it protected me during the 2020 downturn, it has not appreciated much. Although I will get all my money back plus some modest gains in 2027, I would have done better taking the risk of investing the money in the stock market for the past three years. Had I to do it over, I would have stayed away from the annuities altogether.

A Simple Strategy

The above information can be overwhelming. I do not want you to roll your eyes, throw up your hands, and abandon this chapter. Therefore, I offer a simplified strategy that will be effective even if you ignore all the details presented above.

If one has the discipline to save, invest, and control the emotions of greed and fear, I highly recommend doing your own investing. Open an account with a discount brokerage which charges zero fees on self-executed trades. Most offer a free service to give general investing advice (not specific stocks) because they hope someday to persuade you to buy their mutual funds or hire them to manage your money. I have my accounts with Fidelity, get a free annual review (more often if I desire) from a vice president, and have never paid any management fees for 20 years. Earlier, they charged a $6 fee for each trade, but now all trades are free if you personally execute your trades online, not requiring the broker to place them for you. It is extremely easy to place these trades yourself, and no reason to get help, other than an advisor showing you how to trade online initially. So, with a discount brokerage today, you can buy and sell hundreds of stocks, ETFs, and bonds every year without incurring any fees, not that I recommend trading that often.

To keep it simple, allocate a percentage of your portfolio in an ETF equity index fund, such as the S&P 500. Invest six month's salary in a liquid asset that you can withdraw at any time without penalty. Invest the rest in a fixed income ETF, such as FLOT or PCQ. Each month add to this portfolio in the same allocation percentages as above. Adjust this by rebalancing (selling and buying) once per year to maintain the same allocation percentages as above. As you get closer to retirement, change the above allocation to weigh more heavily toward the fixed income. Even with this simple strategy your portfolio should do better than paying someone to manage your money.

Kurth Krause

11. HOUSING CHOICES

Like almost everyone else, we could not afford to buy a home when we first were married. We found a nice three-room apartment that we could easily afford at $105 per month and signed a one-year lease. But with both of us working at professional careers, and able to easily save, having no children and only one car, we were able to buy a small new model home 18 months later for $23,000. This was one of the best decisions we made, placing $7,500 down and securing a 5¼ % mortgage. Four years later, we sold it for a $6,000 profit and bought a 2,500 square-foot home in Texas for $33,000 with a 6% mortgage.

Eight years later, we sold the Texas home for a $22,000 profit and bought a 2,800 square-foot home in Southern California for $88,000. We assumed the buyer's existing eight-year-old 6¼ % mortgage. (The current 1975 bank mortgage rate was in the high teens.) Forty-four years later, we sold this home for almost $1.3 million. Each of these housing decisions served us well. Otherwise we would never have been able to comfortably retire at age 58. The large down payments, our high credit rating (825), the low interest rates, and the inflation of the housing market all played a part. But the income tax deductions for interest and property taxes also helped.

Housing decisions are some of the most important to make, not only financially, but for location, comfort, and peace of mind.

When children are part of the family, making sure the location qualifies for good public schools can be critical. An expensive alternative is a private school. Before we moved to Southern California, my commute to my work was not difficult. But the 33 miles commute to TRW was stressful and taxing because of the traffic. Originally, I vowed not to locate for such a commute, but I relinquished because everything else was perfect: a large, affordable house on a quiet cul-de-sac, near good schools, and two blocks from a great golf course. When I retired 23 years later, the commute problem was resolved forever.

Reata Glen

In June 2019 we decided to move to a Continuing Care Retirement Community (CCRC) in Rancho Mission Viejo, California. Although we were in reasonably good health, we realized this would not always be the case. By moving to a CCRC, our children would not have to deal with any problems we might incur as we continued to age. Reata Glen is new and opened just a month before we moved in. If we ever need it, the campus will have a skilled nursing center, an assisted living center, and a mental health care facility, designed to accommodate 150 people. We are watching its construction just down the hill from our villa. It should be ready this fall if they pass the state regulations.

The Reata Glen complex consists of 78 two- and three-bedroom villas, 76 two- and three-bedroom condominiums called the Garden Terraces, and 326 one- and two- bedroom apartments surrounding the massive clubhouse. Currently, on the first anniversary of its opening, 52% of the units are occupied. Inside the clubhouse are three dining rooms, three card rooms including two poker tables, a pool table, a movie theater, a concert hall/ballroom, a fitness center, a computer lab, a conference room, a salon, a large pool and spa, homemade pastries and coffee each morning, homemade cookies each afternoon, a dance studio, a library, a nurse station with Teladoc service, and an arts and crafts facility. In the adjacent building is a wood-working shop. Outside are tennis courts, pickleball courts, bocce ball, a courtyard with a waterfall fountain and koi pond, and a putting green. There are numerous clubs to join. I now belong to an investment club, which our leader has named the Wizards. I have volunteered for the standing finance committee which is now forming. Unfortunately, during the coronavirus pandemic, many of these facilities are operating under strict safety rules. For the past three months we have been ordering our meals online and the staff has been delivering them to our door. We also order free movies on DVD which provides some entertainment during these trying times.

Reata Glen is expensive, partly due to the ability to move to the on-campus nursing facility if we need it. Since the evening meal is included in our monthly payments, the only additional cost for the special care is the two additional daily meals. So, the high monthly cost is subsidizing any residents requiring the nursing facility, which is currently $15,000 per month for outside patients. If Sue or I never need this facility, we are significantly overpaying for the monthly services. In addition, an exceptionally large lump sum is required for our housing unit. Although we do not own the house, Reata Glen gets 5% of this for each of the first five years. If we vacate any time after five years, 75% of the move-in lump sum is returned. Since Reata Glen owns our house, they pay for all maintenance services, gardening, housekeeping, safety and security, property taxes, utilities, and transportation to local stores, churches, and doctors. Also included are entertainment and community parties during holidays, birthday parties, and special events. They also sponsor several excursions to local venues.

Although the transportation is provided, we pay for any excursion admission fees.

Moving here took a real effort. It took us almost nine months to sell our home in Costa Mesa. After living there for 44 years, moving required major downsizing, going from a five-bedroom 3,200 square-foot home with a three-car garage to a three-bedroom 1,700 square-foot home with a 1½-car garage. We sold Sue's Jaguar and now share my Tesla. But we are thoroughly enjoying our backyard view of the hills, the mountains, and the birds. The people here are wonderful with interesting backgrounds and careers. All are retired; at least one resident must be at least 60 years old. We have had dinner with half of them before the Shelter-in-Place orders were mandated and have made many friends. Even with the shutdown, we still have cocktail parties with people in our backyards.

It is quite satisfying to know our children will not have to deal with our end-of-life problems. We learned that this is the right thing to do for our children and grandchildren from Sue's parents who executed a similar plan for their last few years.

In retrospect, I do not regret any housing decision and would not want to do anything differently than we did. However, one decision did cost us financially. If we had sold our California home after it appreciated $500,000, we would have avoided all capital gains taxes because currently the IRS tax law excludes the first $500,000 gain on a home sale. But we may not have found a home as ideally suited to replace it. Also, our property taxes would have increased by more than $10,000 per year.

12. INSURANCE TRADEOFFS

Everyone buys insurance because we cannot afford the possible out-of-pocket losses, right? Not necessarily. If medical insurance is paid for or at least subsidized by your employer, as was mine, of course you buy it. But what if you are in private business by yourself? You may be better off not buying it. In fact, home insurance, life insurance, auto insurance, and liability insurance may not be right for you. You may be insurance poor. Let me explain.

I took a course in risk management, taught by a self-employed man married to an infirmed wife. He made the point that we all are too risk-averse, and our decisions are costing us personally as well as our employer. Consider how insurance works. Insurance companies make a fortune because the claims are much less than the premiums. The premiums not only cover the claims, but the overhead, the agent's commissions, the millions spent on TV ads, and the handsome profits realized by these giant companies. If we find a way to take the risks ourselves and are self-insured, these commissions, overhead, and profit are ours to keep because we do not pay any premiums. Of course, this means that we are incurring risk that our claims may greatly exceed the savings we built up over the years by not paying premiums. But that is exactly the bet that works so well for the insurance companies.

To take such risks, we must have built up a war chest of liquid assets to cover the potential losses. We challenged the self-employed risk management instructor by asking whether he actually put this strategy into practice personally. To my astonishment he said he did, He was self-insured with no auto, no life, no home, even no medical insurance with his quadriplegic wife. Obviously, he did have sufficient liquid assets to be self-insured. He had to put up a bond to satisfy the state requirement to cover auto liability. I gave this a lot of thought and took some action. I cancelled my life insurance, (It is foolish to pay for whole life instead of term, unless you don't have the discipline to save enough.), took the maximum deduction on my auto insurance, and did the same on my homeowner's policy. My liquid assets were significant, but I did not have the courage to drop my home and auto insurance completely. But I did realize that had I experienced a financial catastrophe, such as losing my home to fire, or my car to an accident, these losses would be tax deductible. In retrospect, I could have saved substantial money over the past 50 years by dropping my home insurance entirely and putting up a bond to cover my mortgage balance. As my assets grew, however, I significantly increased my liability insurance because lawsuits could be prohibitively expensive. So, I bought a two-million-dollar policy for liability. I will probably never have to make a claim, but the $244 per year premium lets me sleep at night.

My father believed in insurance to the extreme of becoming insurance poor. Eventually he cashed in his whole life policy. After he retired, I tried to convince him that paying $5,000 per year for a policy to supplement Medicare was a bad idea. He tried to convince me it was worthwhile by showing me the medical bills that were covered. But he did not believe me when I pointed out that these bills were paid by Medicare, not the supplement. In my opinion, insurance companies realize great profits from all medical insurance, which means the premiums greatly exceed the average claims. I believe everyone who does not have medical insurance covered by their employer or the government should only buy catastrophic insurance to cover the major cash outlays for operations and long-term hospital stays. Similarly, it may be folly to pay premiums to cover long-term care if you have sufficient assets. As you get older, these premiums escalate prohibitively. I have a friend who carried these policies for decades but had to drop them when the premium got too high. Some of these insurers have stopped selling these policies because they had to escalate long-term care premiums to prohibitive levels to cover their claims.

When we bought our home in Southern California, we were afraid of earthquakes, so we added earthquake insurance to our homeowner's policy. But when a major earthquake hit the San Fernando Valley in 1994 and premiums went up along with deductibles, I dropped the policy. I also learned some insurers went out of business to avoid paying the claims.

13. RETIREMENT FINANCES

How much do I need to retire?

      This is an important investment issue. Usually it is a great deal more than one expects. According to Phil Town's book *Payback Time*, by 2030 you will need $3 million to retire comfortably. The expected rate of return of one's investments is critical. The problem is that it is a mistake to use an average rate of return each year. Obviously if one uses an 8 % average return on stocks every year, but the market goes down 40% one year, then up 56% the next to average 8%, the result is a 6.4% loss for the two years, rather than an annual rate of 8% compounded into a total gain of 16.64% for the two years. The amount of expenditures required each year is easier to forecast once we pick a rate of inflation. I built a computer model to determine whether we could afford our current lifestyle through our retirement years. I assumed our only assured income would be our Social Security escalated by the rate of inflation each year. All other expenditures would come from our investments. I assumed a rate of inflation of 4% each year, which is almost 1% higher than historical averages. I assumed that once we reach 85 our lifestyle would be less costly: high medical costs (perhaps even assisted living), but much less travel, entertainment, and golf. For investment rate of return, I used historical year-by-year results for the past 35 years for both stocks and bonds. Then I carried this out to see the year-by-year results on a spreadsheet. It is interesting to note that by reducing the rate of inflation to 2% I could see my investments grow indefinitely even after spending at a rate to maintain our lifestyle. But by using a high inflation rate (4%), my portfolio would eventually go to zero. So, inflation, investment growth, and expenditure rate have a profound effect on when your money will run out.

Planning for retirement is a financial difficulty. It would be easier if you knew how long you and your spouse would live. Your sources of income after you retire include your liquid assets (stocks, bonds, certificates of deposit and cash), IRA, Social Security, and pension, if any. I elected to take my pension as a lump sum for me to invest as part of my IRA. I reasoned that this could be safely invested, tax deferred, increased with inflation, and I would not have to reduce the payments to include my wife. In retrospect, this was a mistake. Investments can be volatile, which is particularly a problem if I did not have enough time to make up for significant losses, such as experienced in 2001, 2009, and 2020. The only risk to the monthly pension was that TRW would go out of business and be bankrupt, an extremely unlikely scenario. Although the monthly payments would be fixed and not changed with inflation, they were based on the 1999 interest rate of 6% and my estimated longevity. They would be paid no matter how long I lived. Given that today's interest rates are less than 3%, inflation has been less than 2%, and I am now in good health and 79 years-old, it would have been better to take this guaranteed monthly income of approximately $300. I would have to pay ordinary income tax annually on this money, while the IRA is tax deferred, but the peace of mind that it was guaranteed income would have been welcomed.

Since I had contributed the maximum allowed throughout my career, I built a significant IRA portfolio. But now I must pay income tax on the Required Minimum Distribution every year at the higher tax rate.

Social Security

I also made a calculated error in deciding to begin taking my Social Security at age 63. Sue was concerned that our longevity might not be above average. She is a cancer survivor and has a legacy of defective kidneys, so she started taking her SS at age 62. I was concerned that the government might exhaust SS funding in a few years, so I stated taking payments at age 63. Had we waited until age 70, we would now be receiving 7.4% more per month for the rest of our lives. I wish that wise little bird would have advised me on these decisions—a lesson learned too late. One problem is that 85% of the SS funds are taxable on the Federal returns. Fortunately, my IRA funds should easily last the rest of our lives, provided the stocks and bonds act appropriately. One decision that may work to our benefit is that we created a tax-free Roth IRA for some of our assets.

14. TRAVELING THE WORLD

I had no idea that traveling would add so much to my life. We traveled little while we had children. High cost, minimal vacation time, and complexity dealing with a family of four constrained us. We did follow through on our promise to visit my parents and grandparents in Milwaukee annually, but we always stayed in our parents' homes, and except when we moved to California, always drove, rather than flew. But these trips did not inspire us to travel.

When Sheryl left for college, we acquired our first passports and began to travel extensively for pleasure. To date, we have visited 99 countries and 75 islands, and we have taken 41 cruises. I offer this synopsis of the highlights of our travel in hopes you are inspired to experience some of them.

Italy

Our first international trip was a three-week land tour of Italy with American Express. We were enthralled with the small medieval cities like Verona, Siena, and San Gimignano. Romantic Tuscany captured our hearts, and Florence did not disappoint; I even enjoyed the Uffizi Art Gallery. Seeing the Leaning Tower of Pisa impressed me when I remembered that it was here that Galileo dropped two balls of significantly different mass to prove that gravity caused them to descend at the same rate, independent of weight.

The Pompeii site amazed me. Much of it seemed perfectly preserved when buried by the ash from Mt. Vesuvius' eruptions in 79 AD. Multicolored murals on so many walls were uncovered. The amount of pornography and the phallic symbols carved into the pathway to the brothel surprised me.

I have fond memories of the Vatican's Sistine Chapel, the Colosseum, the Trevi Fountain, the Spanish Steps, the Catacombs, and the Forum of Rome. The sixteenth century gardens and estate, Villa d' Este, in Tivoli impressed me. The owner had rerouted a river through the property to create innumerable fountains everywhere on his land.

In the Italian Alps we viewed arguably the three most beautiful lakes in the world: Lake Lugano, Lake Como, and Lake Maggiore. Of course, we also toured Milan. There we saw, just two feet in front of us, the original Leonardo da Vinci mural of *The Last Supper* on the end wall of the dining hall at the Monastery of Santa Maria delle Grazie. I could hardly believe it.

China

Shortly thereafter, we booked a land tour of China, which was eye-opening. In Shanghai, Sue and I left the group to venture into a park next to our hotel. We were the only Americans, surrounded by Chinese practicing Tai Chi and just enjoying the park. China had just been opened to tourists, so it appeared many were not accustomed to foreigners in their little park. Sue drew a crowd around her. They were fascinated by her blond hair. Two professors tried out their newly learned English on us. One of them sold us some local post cards.

In Beijing, we were impressed by the vast Tiananmen Square with the large poster of Mao Tse-tung prominently and centrally displayed at one end. We explored the forbidden city, noticing the little two- and three-year-old boys dressed like royalty with their cute little red caps. We were thrilled to walk on the Great Wall of China.

We sailed a Chinese junk boat down the Li River in Guilin. More than one hundred limestone "thumbs" up to 200 feet high, rising through the mist on the river made this surrealistic.

We flew to Xian to see the famous Terra Cotta Warriors. Although there were only 2,000 figures uncovered (8,000 today) the scene was impressive. They were created 2,200 years ago to defend China's first emperor in the afterlife and are buried in four pits less than one mile from the emperor's tomb. Although the bodies were cast from a few standard molds (standing, kneeling, driving a horse-drawn chariot), all their faces are different, carved by hand. But there was so much pollution in Xian that almost all the residents wore facemasks.

We learned from the Italy and China trips how to improve our international travel experience. The American Express tour endured a full bus load of 40 people. This distracted from our walking tours as well as the lengthy time disembarking, waiting for stragglers, and re-boarding. We discovered a tour agency that met our needs for our future land tours: Overseas Adventure Travel (OAT). This organization guaranteed that our group would never be larger than 16 travelers. We took eight different tours with them and loved each one. We also took one special Tauck tour, which was more upscale, but had 24 people in the group.

Traveling on Our Own

The first time we tried international travel on our own was rather adventurous. I had accumulated several hundred thousand business miles on United Airlines by flying to my offices in Houston and Seattle and to our corporate headquarters in Boston. Now it was time to use these miles effectively. We flew first class on our first five trips to Asia and Europe using these free miles. First, we decided to explore two exotic cities in Asia which sounded adventurous: Singapore and Hong Kong on a single trip. And indeed, they were.

Singapore and Hong Kong

It took more than 18 hours to get to Singapore, but first class made it enjoyable: luxurious seats, great service, top-shelf cocktails, chilled vodka, excellent food, and pampering. I could get used to this! We spent five days in Singapore with a multiday bus pass, visiting zoo and museums, shopping on Orchard Street, having a Singapore Sling at Raffle's, and exploring Sentosa Island via a cable car from the World Trade Center. Two unusual things struck us: the absolute cleanliness of all the streets and the sparsity of people. We learned we would be fined $500 to spit out gum anywhere.

Remarkably, this island city was reclaiming land from the ocean, building new upscale hotels (Our new Westin was only 1/3 full.), beginning to build their Mass Rapid Transit system, and enhancing their infrastructure. It seemed a foolish extravagance to me. Now I realize they were prophetic with these major investments, as Singapore would soon become a magnet for adventurous world travelers. We have returned three more times in our travels.

Hong Kong, the Pearl of the Orient, lived up to its nickname. We visited prior to Great Britain returning control of Hong Kong to China. Its vibrant economy, great shopping bargains, interesting people, and beautiful, vibrant harbor viewed from Victoria Peak made this one of my favorite cities in the world. We stayed in the Hyatt on the Kowloon side of the harbor.

We took the 50-minute Russian hydrofoil to Macau for a few hours. At that time, it was a favorite place to gamble for the Chinese in Hong Kong. The housewives would go there for the day while their husbands were at work. Today it is the gambling capital of the world, surpassing Las Vegas.

Back in Hong Kong, we shopped 'til we dropped, buying jewelry, tailored new suits, and $20 four-ply cashmere sweaters for everyone we knew. The tailor sent a bottle of Chivas Regal to our hotel as a thank you. We bought another large suitcase to haul it all home. Since that trip, we returned to Hong Kong three more times, but it has changed since becoming part of China in 1997. The people did not seem as energetic, and the prices were much higher.

France, Germany, and Switzerland

The first time we traveled to France, Germany, and Switzerland, we also ventured out on our own. We spent four days exploring Paris, rented a car to discover Bavaria's Black Forest, the Swiss and French Alps, then down to Monaco and the French Riviera.

Paris was magical. We stayed in a two-story walkup, halfway between the Arc de Triomphe and the Eiffel Tower. We could see both from our room. We explored Paris, riding their excellent Metro lines as well as on foot. Most impressive were the Seine, the Notre-Dame Cathedral, the Louvre, the Eiffel Tower, Concord Square, the curbside cafes and coffee shops, the quaint shops and bookstores along the Right Bank of the Seine, and the narrow historic streets.

As a special treat, we decided to experience a Michelin Two Star restaurant. We dressed up as best we could muster with our traveling clothes, hopped on to the Metro and got off on the Champs Elysees, noticing the Bentleys dropping impeccably dressed people, some in military dress uniforms, at our restaurant. We calmly walked in like we belonged there and were seated by our tuxedo-clad waiter. With our Berlitz book, we tried to decipher the menu. Sue recognized "canard" and ordered the duck with a salad and green beans. The waiter vehemently objected, pointing out that the green beans did not properly go with her entrée choice. Although we were not wine drinkers, we ordered the bottle of wine he suggested. After going through the first course, drinking several glasses of wine, we were feeling no pain when the entrees arrived. Sue's duck looked strange: two large slabs of exceptionally smooth meat. She liked it, not tasting like duck, but familiar. It was duck liver! The waiter pointed out the large ducks in cages. Well we finished the wine with our entrees and ordered another half bottle to go with our Gran Marnier Souffle. Fortunately, we were taking the metro home, or we might not have made it.

We spent an unforgettable day touring Versailles. The palace itself is breathtaking with its hall of mirrors, gold, crystal, and precious gem adornments, the Royal Chapel, and the amazing artwork. The vast gardens of Versailles impressed us with the rare flowers, sculptures, and fountains.

The next day we rented our car, a stick-shift Renault, and left Paris for the German Black Forest. After driving through beautiful Freiberg, we approached the little town of Triberg. We had to park our car outside the town. They were having their own little Octoberfest and no traffic was allowed. We followed the residents to their party and joined in, although we could not speak a word of German. Picnic tables were laid out in front of the food booths. We made our selections including the traditional Black Forest Cake and sat down with the Germans. I pointed to a man's stein of beer and animatedly asked where I could buy the beer. He got up and took me by the hand to the beer booth. An old-fashioned organ grinder was entertaining us with his pet monkey. This was a memorable stop on our journey through the Black Forest.

We drove our little French car down through the majestic Swiss Alps. We toured the Swiss heritage sites in Interlaken and spent the night on the shore of Lake Lucerne, viewing the historic bridges on the Reuss River. We longed to replace the German food with French cooking, so we headed back into France at Lyon. We took full advantage of our Michelin Guide to find great French restaurants, denoted by the red *R* next to the name of the hotel. There we spent the night, usually in a spartan three-story walk-up, hauling our luggage. But the hotel was usually owned by a renowned chef, retired from Paris, whose meals were exquisite. I remember paying $80 for dinner and $20 for the room. Both were priced right. In the morning, we would stop at little stores for bread, cheese, salami, and bakery. Then, with our newly acquired taste, we would buy a bottle of red wine for our lunch, all of which we consumed off the road. I remember how friendly the merchants in these towns were, helping us struggle with our French and congratulating us when we got it right. So different from the rude Parisians.

When we finally made it down to the Mediterranean, we toured up and down the Riviera, noting the difference in their beaches. Our hotel room in Nice overlooked these beaches, which instead of sand was smooth stones and pebbles. At lunch time we witnessed French women in business suits stripping off all their clothes to don bikini bottoms in preparation for their hour in the sun.

Of course, we drove up to beautiful Monaco and gambled at Monte Carlo, where I won five francs playing blackjack. But I absentmindedly drove down a street for pedestrians only. So, Sue took over the driving as we made our way up the mountainside overlooking Monaco. We wanted to get off this treacherous narrow two-lane mountain road to get back to Nice before sunset, but there were no turnoffs. We were relieved to see a sign that indicated to stay on the same road to reach the highway. So, Sue struggled with the Renault's stick shift on the three scenic corniches before reaching the top of the mountain. (Never again did we rent a stick shift.)

On our last day, we became spectators for an Ironman Triathlon on the beach in front of our hotel. Here the start of the 2.4-mile ocean swim began. After the swim, the contestants stripped off their swimsuits to get into their racing togs for the 112-mile bicycle leg which finished at the starting place before beginning the 26.2-mile run. We could not watch the finish, as we had to catch our flight back to the US.

Kurth Krause

Australia

We booked our own trip to Australia, a 14-hour flight to Sydney, connecting to Cairns in Queensland. We began with a tour of the Daintree rainforest in a DUKW or "duck," a six-wheeled amphibious 2½ ton WWII truck. This adventure fascinated us, spotting the unique species of flora and fauna in the dense, overcrowded rainforest floor. Then we boarded a 69-passenger boat, the Coral Princess, for a four-day cruise on the unique Great Barrier Reef and its islands. We had to delay our Australian trip one week because the boat was in dry dock waiting for a new propeller. We had only 36 passengers on board and a 25-year-old captain, the youngest in Australia. We were the only Americans, mostly Brits, Kiwis, and a few Germans. This trip both exhilarated and exhausted us, snorkeling on the reef every day, eating fresh seafood, including spiny lobsters, and fresh fruit. I was up in the bridge with the captain when we navigated our last leg into Townsville, our final destination. He had the throttle wide open for the last few miles, as I noticed the tide going out and the sonar showing three, then two, then one, then ½ meter clearance! I surmised that this was why the last captain was fired: he ran aground and bent the propeller.

At Townsville we caught a flight to Brisbane on Australia's Gold Coast, connecting to Sydney. There we stayed at the Hyatt in Kings Cross in the Red-Light District, conveniently located to the Sydney Metro rapid transit system. The underground Metro was delightful, with musicians entertaining at some stops, including ours at the Kings Cross Station. We took the Metro to the Sydney Opera house for a concert, to the half-price ticket booths, and to the musical plays, which we thoroughly enjoyed. We also took day trips out of Sydney to the Blue Mountains and the outback. Most of all we enjoyed meeting real Aussies, quite friendly and interested in Americans. A national pastime is consuming their lager beer, principally Fosters, which we learned to down like a native. After all, we had to reciprocate their friendliness.

New Zealand

Seven months later, we embarked on another self-reliant adventure to delightful New Zealand. We had heard how great the Kiwi people are, so we decided to try the bed and breakfast route. Based on travel agent bookings, the price of these accommodations seemed high. But the wise bird on my shoulder advised us to wait until we arrived and book locally directly with the locals. So, we took a chance by advance booking only the first few days with the Hyatt chain, with which we had a frequent traveler discount, and leaving the rest of our itinerary open.

Once again, we flew the 14-hour, first class flight to Auckland, stayed at the Hyatt, and rented a car (with an automatic transmission). It would be hard enough to negotiate the wrong side of the road without the trauma of manipulating a stick shift. The first thing we did was to find the right bookshop to buy the guide to bed and breakfast places throughout the country. (Airbnb did not surface until twenty years later.) The wise bird was right again; the prices were a small fraction of what the agent quoted in the US. And the book described each domicile and its host in quaint detail, down to the description and name of its pets. We also purchased a NZ telephone card to enable booking the rest of our reservations.

The next day we drove to Rotorua, where were learned about the fascinating Maori. The Maori are the indigenous people who arrived from Polynesia during the 14th century. They are dark skinned with colorful clothing and elaborate skin decorations and tattoos. Although they brought their own culture of mythology, crafts, and performing arts, the Europeans arriving 400-600 years later influenced their culture, enabling a degree of coexistence. We found them quite friendly and admired their craftsman skills, especially in building canoes.

A direct descendent of a Maori chief guided us through the famous Waitomo glowworm cave on the central part of the North Island, 87 miles from Rotorua. The glowworms are unique in the world. We relaxed and laid back in a boat, floating through the cave's stream and looking up at the thousands of these creatures hanging from the cave's ceilings and lighting our way.

We drove to Wellington, New Zealand's capitol, at the southern tip of the North Island. En route we experienced first-hand the fact that there were seven times more sheep than people. Several times we had to stop the car to let the sheep cross the road. The owner checked us in to her B&B, then offered to take us on a tour of the town, of which she was immensely proud.

The next morning, we dropped off our rental car to board the Cook Strait Ferry to take us to the South Island. This strait is considered one of the most dangerous and unpredictable waters in the world, although it is only 14 miles wide. It connects the Tasmanian Sea with the South Pacific Ocean. Our ferry only spent half the time in the strait, the rest of the three-hour, 43-mile journey in the Marlboro Sounds, docking at Picton. We were lucky to cross in good weather and made friends with two young Kiwi sailors onboard. We picked up our next rental car and gave our new friends a lift to Christ Church.

Christ Church is in the Canterbury Region on the South Island's east coast. Although it is New Zealand's second largest city, it seemed like a delightful, quaint small town, designed around the central Cathedral Square. It became a city in 1856, laid out in a grid pattern around the square. We were saddened when it suffered a series of major earthquakes during 2010-2012, demolishing 1,500 buildings and killing 185. It is still being rebuilt today. While staying in Christ Church we spent one morning taking a helicopter ride around the spectacular glaciers of Mount Cook. It was expensive but so worth it.

The next day we motored south to the little town of Dunedin. We stopped to see the Royal Albatross Colony on the Otago Peninsula. This is the world's only mainland breeding colony for these special birds, who spend 85% of their lives at sea. We were able to approach them, astonished as to their size, weighing 22 pounds with a wingspan of up to 11 feet. I was in awe, watching them take off and land on the treacherous cliffs. They soar much like a glider. They are so big that they need the high winds on these cliffs to get airborne. That evening we paid $3 to enter a farmer's land to view the penguins coming in from the sea to their nests. Rain was pouring down, and they were so far from our cliff viewpoint that they were hard to see.

The next day, driving farther south and inland, we reached exiting Queenstown. As we approached, we stopped to view people bungee jumping off the Kawarau bridge, where the sport originated in 1979. The brave jumpers are weighed to determine how much slack is required to stop just above the river's surface, some 142 feet down. One of the staff told us they used to allow the females to jump free of charge if they jumped in the nude. But they stopped offering the freebies when they had so many girls jumping that they lost money. Although we declined on this, the first of a triad of events called the Super Triple Challenge (bungee jumping, sky diving and hang gliding), we did participate in the less crazy standard triple challenge: Shotover River jet boat ride, helicopter through Skipper's Canyon, and whitewater river rafting at Deep Creek. As we neared the final stretch of rafting, the river became a Class V, and we had to hold on for dear life. They took our picture from the shore to capture the fear on our faces, but we were going backward and flying at the time. In our wetsuits, life jackets, and helmets, we resembled Ninja Turtles. We stayed three nights in this fun, adventurous town, feeling old compared to the twentysomethings that dominated. We did take a more sedate boat trip through beautiful Milford Sound and its amazing waterfall before flying to Auckland for the trip home.

Spain

Spain was much more than we anticipated. After a few days in Madrid, where we spent two days at the Prado, we rented a car to drive a loop around southern Spain, ending back in Madrid. But we were warned to examine the tires of the rental before we started driving. Thieves posing as good Samaritans will make cuts in a tire, and when we stopped to change the flat, they will offer to help as they rob us. We stayed in paradors, luxury hotels that the government renovated at historical monasteries and castles or in locations with exceptional topography and view.

We drove to Toledo, an UNESCO World Heritage Site, and the medieval "Imperial City" that was the capital of the province from 542 to 725 AD. Our parador overlooked the city. Throughout Toledo are markings showing the route of mythical Don Quixote. Next, we drove down to Granada to see the Alhambra. The small parador here had no vacancy, so we had to drive 38 miles up a winding mountain road to stay in a parador at the Sierra Nevada Ski Station. The Alhambra is an Arab citadel and palace. It is the most famous building in Moorish Islamic history.

We then drove down to the Costa del Sol in Andalusia. We stopped in Malaga to shop, but when the proprietor learned we were driving a rental car, he told us to immediately get back to our car or the trunk will be forced open and our suitcase stolen. We crossed over a bridge to the British island of Gibraltar, where we bought the Lladro Flower Girl piece that Sue had admired for years. It cost $2,500 at home, but only $1,000 in Gibraltar due in part to zero value added tax. The problem now was to get it home in one piece. As we drove up the Gibraltar grades, the car was inundated by monkeys, and we were happy to get back to town in one piece.

We drove along the coast looking up the high cliffs to the beautiful white cities of Andalusia until we reached Cadiz and Valencia. We loved the environs of Valencia, but kept our windows closed and dared not stop, as we were told of thieves that zip by on mopeds to snatch purses or anything loose off our bodies as they race by. We did spend one night on the southern coast of Portugal, but it was unremarkable compared to the grandeur of Spain.

We stopped at Merida, the Spanish Roman capital in 25 AD. We were surprised by the excellent condition of the Roman ruins, second only to Rome. Notable were the Puente Romano, the oldest existing Roman bridge, the Forum, the Temple of Diana, the Circus Maximus, the Amphitheater, and the National Museum of Roman Art, containing wonderful Roman artifacts.

We drove north to discover the city of Avila, 3700 feet above sea level. It is surrounded by medieval walls where several movies were filmed. It is another UNESCO World Heritage Site.

We drove only 40 miles east to explore the small city of Segovia. It sports a magnificent fairy castle, the Alcazar of Segovia, which looked quite familiar; it was a template for Disney's Cinderella Castle. Another great landmark is the 2500-foot-long first century Roman aqueduct with 170 arches, another UNESCO World Heritage Site.

When we returned to Madrid, Air Force One held up our flight, as George Bush landed to visit the prime minister of Spain.

All Inclusive Resorts

Acapulco

After visiting a Club Med for dinner in Kauai, we decided to try one in Mexico, just North of Acapulco. Spartan accommodations and unremarkable cuisine enabled low cost, but it was pure fun. We were in our thirties, still young enough to mingle with the younger couples and staff, called GOs. We played tennis, learned how to sail in a one-man Sunflower, snorkeled, and bought drinks with plastic beads around our necks so we did not need pockets in our swimsuits. While enjoying the beautiful sunsets, we would get an umbrella drink, sit back in our hammocks, and watch the pelicans fly in time to the classical music on the speakers. It was magical. Every night we would all gather before dinner to sing and dance to their crazy songs, like the chicken dance and *YMCA*. But mid-week the Mexican Federales confiscated our windsurfing boards because Club Med would not pay the $100 per board bribe to get them returned. They confiscated all the tennis balls the week before for the same reason. But we had so much fun, we decided to do another.

On our way home our plane was late, missing our connection in Mexico City. So, we had to spend the night. Mexican Airlines would not reimburse us, so someone from the Holiday Inn offered to give us a package deal for $200 per person. I asked the airline attendant if we could get something cheaper. We took a $2 cab ride to a hotel in a poor part of town. We had an excellent meal, drinks, and a nice room for a total of $35 for the two of us! Lesson learned: do not accept an unsolicited accommodation deal at an airport just because it is convenient.

Playa Blanca

A few years later we convinced our friends, Don and Vanda, to join us at the Club Med in Playa Blanca, Mexico. It was equally enjoyable. We started with a bus ride from the Mazatlán airport. The Club Med bus stopped in town to "stock up" with Tequila and beer for the two-hour trek over a narrow, dangerous dirt road.

Vanda instantly loved it as, upon arrival, we immediately got into our swim gear and almost never wore anything else the whole week. Playa Blanca was just as spartan with twin beds and straw mattresses. This time Sue and I knew all the songs and dances, which added to our enjoyment. This club was primarily couples, often unmarried, as we learned by their clothes optional solarium and beach. The rooms only locked from the inside. We heard the girl next door trying to get her roommate and her boyfriend to open the door so she could retrieve her clothes for the night. One night we learned about tequila "slammers" which we all tried before playing volleyball by spotlight. We rode horses along the beach, slowly on the way out and extremely fast on the way back. We had fun going deep sea fishing, but of course Sue caught all the fish. We decided another Club Med was in our future.

Paradise Island

Once again, Don and Vanda joined us for a Club Med on Paradise Island across from Nassau in the Bahamas. This was a little more upscale, but still inexpensive. One thing we did was quite different here. We took an excursion off campus, where we each donned an old-fashioned diving helmet connected to a land-based air tube, went 15 feet under water, walked along the bottom of the sea, and stood still with our arms extended as a giant grouper swam into our arms and posed for the picture. Club Med was located adjacent to the new Atlantis Resort. So, we were able to play some blackjack before we flew home.

Puerto Rico

We joined Sue's parents at El Conquistador, a beautiful resort on the east end of Puerto Rico. The hotel is located on a 300-foot cliff overlooking the Caribbean, but one can take a fun funicular down the cliff to reach the beach and golf course. We loved it there, playing golf and beaching. But one day Sue insisted on going to see the San Juan racetrack. Reluctantly, the four of us hired a taxi to take us 40 miles to the other end of the island in hot, humid weather. I learned that the Hipódromo Camarero track "take" was much higher than the 17% seized on the US horse racetracks. Sue made it a point to go down to the track to look over the steeds to scientifically pick out the winners of each race. She did. Every one of her eight picks finished dead last, except one—he finished second last. When we told the taxi driver on the way back, he could not stop laughing, claiming that had to be a record.

Dominican Republic

We joined Sue's sister, Sandy, and brother-in-law, John for a strange itinerary to get to the all-inclusive Excellence Resort in Punta Cana. We left balmy Southern California to fly to Winneconne, Wisconsin in February to join their group. So, we wore our winter coats to go to a tropical climate in the Caribbean. The group was fun, so it was worth it—maybe? The great resort offered six restaurants, upscale liquor, and an enormous pool. We played a few silly, but fun games. Sue and I managed to capsize a catamaran sailboat and had to be rescued. We took a tour of the island to break the monotony. The week was laid back and slow-moving.

Jamaica

We spent a more active week at the Breezes Resort in Ocho Rios with Sandy and John. We always enjoy John and Sandy's company. We were able to play 36 holes of golf. We got soaked negotiating the water trek up Dunn's River Falls, walking uphill against the river current. It was reminiscent of the first time we visited Breezes on our own, a beautiful, romantic place.

Guided Land Tours

Our trips with a professional guide were every bit as enjoyable as the land trips we did on our own. Most of these were with Overseas Adventure Travel (OAT), which guarantees a group with never more than 16 passengers. This feature, their excellent guides, and the promise of adventure always made these trips memorable. Visiting the local schools and homes gave an insight into their cultures that would not be possible in a large group. In addition, sharing the adventures with a small group enabled closer relationships with one's fellow travelers.

Thailand

Our first trip with OAT was two weeks in Thailand. Our guide was a young man, who served two months in a monastery as a celibate, ordained Buddhist monk prior to his marriage, as was required in the Thai culture. Ninety percent of all Thai are Buddhists. This explains why we were shown so many wats (temples) and statues of Buddha in various positions, some of which were extraordinary (e.g., the emerald Buddha made entirely of jade, the 300 foot giant sitting Buddha, the 150 foot reclining Nirvana Buddha, and the solid gold Buddha).

Bangkok is one of the world's most fascinating cities with dazzling temples, a world-famous floating market, spectacular palaces, shrines, a colorful Chinatown, and much humidity. We rode several longtail boats (I called them the sore tail boats.) with outboard motors to get around the crowded city much more efficiently than any other type of transportation. We dined at interesting restaurants with scrumptious seafood but also dined with a Thai family in their home My three-hour massage recommended by our guide was not pleasant. An extravaganza of the Siam Niramit show dazzled us the final night before we motored north to explore the famous Bridge over the River Kwai and the Death Railway. Unfortunately, we viewed the corresponding museum of the macabre conditions imposed by the Japanese on the allied WWII POWs.

Then we continued north to the majestic mountainous Golden Triangle near Chiang Rei on the border of Laos and Burma (now Myanmar). This used to be the location of the largest poppy region for opioids and heroin in the world. We then traveled to Chiang Mei for a one-hour ride on an elephant. Like the other travelers in our group, we bought a bunch of bananas to feed the elephant. He knew we had them, so he continued searching through our shirts with his trunk. If he found the bunch, he would devour it whole, but by feeding him one-at-a-time, he would peel each with his dexterous trunk before stuffing it into his mouth. We thoroughly enjoyed the ride on this gentle giant through the jungle and across a river. We dismounted at an elephant camp where they put on a show for us. The next day we flew back to Bangkok for the long flight home.

Costa Rica

OAT surprised us with a real adventure in Costa Rica. Costa Rica is easily the most developed of the Central American countries. Its major industries include manufacturing of integrated circuits. Our guide was an amateur astronomer, who loved to show us the night sky. He took us through the Costa Rica mountains and jungles, pointing out the unique birds, plants, and trees. The long line of giant black ants crossing our path, each with a leaf segment bigger than its body on its back, was particularly impressive. Our guide explained that they were taking food to their nest, would chew and store it, then eat it during the winter.

The 16 of us boarded a small open-air boat and were introduced to a river guide. We encountered many beautiful native butterflies along the river, including the famous Blue Morpho, one of the largest and most recognizable in the world. There were several crocodiles in the river. When we approached a 16-foot crock which the guide seemed to recognize, he turned the boat and headed to the bank. He disembarked and started slapping the water with the dressed half chicken which he brought along, while backing up toward the bank. The swimming crock made a right-angle turn, heading for the guide double time. He continued to back up while the crocodile fixated on him and the chicken, When the crock opened his gigantic mouth just inches from the guide, the guide let go of the chicken. The crocodile slammed his jaws shut with the chicken inside and took off down the river. I asked the guide about the large scar on his leg. He explained that once there were two crocodiles!

Our guide took us in his 20-passenger van to the base of a semi-active volcano, called Poas, which has erupted dozens of times since 1828. After driving to the base, we climbed up the last part of the rim to almost 7,000 feet to peer over the edge of the cauldron in which a pool of emerald green water collected in the center. Steam escaped around the sides of the pool, a frightening sight.

Our next adventure experienced rafting in one of the best whitewater rivers in the world. We donned our life jackets and received our paddles as we took on two more guides in our two inflatable rafts. At first the river was reasonably calm, enabling us to enjoy the lush vegetation as we paddled through the rainforest. Midway, we stopped for lunch. The two guides went into the forest and came out with two small colorful frogs in their hands. While they appeared cute and attractive, the guides explained they were deadly. Natives would just touch the frogs' backs with their darts and use blow guns to kill their enemies on contact. Yes, they did wash their hands before serving us lunch. Back into the rafts for a rougher ride down the river, but still fun.

We drove to our hotel near Costa Rica's most active volcano, Arenal. It is striking, rising 5,437 feet above the surrounding flatland. It erupts almost daily, and for us it did not disappoint. That evening we witnessed a spectacular eruption, setting the night sky aglow.

Sue and our friend, Mike, decided to join the more adventurous of the group to trek up 1,000 feet to get on a zipline through the forest. Mike's wife, Merle, and I decided to take a safer option and have a massage. Sue loved it. She ziplined down through 11 stations, coming nose-to-nose with howler monkeys in the trees. Our massage was not as much fun as we got manhandled by a blind masseuse.

We mounted horses and rode to the mud baths. We drank beer while mud bathing in the warm springs, then showered to get the mud off. At the end of the day, we rode the horses back to our camp, observing tree sloths along the way.

The final full day ended with our guide and driver taking us to a pinnacle in the Palo Verde National Park, overlooking the Pacific Ocean for a spectacular view. There we spotted a pair of the rare and endangered scarlet macaws. The plumage of these overgrown parrots is striking and can be easily seen from a distance. But there they were, perched in a tree less than 100 feet away. To top off the evening, our guide hooked up some opera music to a speaker in the van and passed out a local coffee liqueur called Britt. Perfect!

Then we had our farewell dinner. We were all jazzed up for a good time. Sue and I take two small, portable three-legged chairs with us wherever we go. This enables us to sit directly in front of the guide to listen to his narrative without blocking the view of our fellow travelers. But this guide did not like it. None of us could figure out why. So, while we were all drinking and having a great time, we commanded the guide and driver to sit in our two chairs as if they were in the van, while we roasted them unmercifully. Everyone thoroughly enjoyed this event except the guide.

Ireland

We teamed up with Mike and Merle and another couple, Al and Luray, to take an OAT trip through Ireland. We spent the entire two weeks touring the scenic southwest part of the island, mostly in County Cork and County Kerry. Our female guide loved her country as did we by the time we completed the tour. Our driver introduced us to Guinness, which eventually I liked. We ended up buying him a pint wherever we went. Of course, we visited the 600-year-old Blarney Castle, but I refused to kiss the Blarney Stone when they told me that 1,000 people do it every day. (Today, it is disinfected each day.) Plus, it was a little scary for someone with a fear of heights since you had to be held upside down three stories up to do so. It was enough to negotiate the narrow spiral staircase to get up there.

We visited the Jameson distillery in Middleton, County Cork, where Merle and I volunteered to try six different kinds of whiskey. Then Merle convinced them to add a seventh: their expensive blend of Irish whiskey. We were feeling no pain the rest of the day.

We toured the bustling town of Killarney and stopped at a pub for our first pint of Guinness, carefully poured to ensure the foam is settled and skimmed off in order to fill the pint to the brim with pure Guinness. In Kearney National Park, we toured the impressive stately Muckross House. We explored several castles and learned why the Irish hated the English, reflecting the destruction performed by Cornwallis and his troops in the 18th century.

Mike, Al, and I attempted to play golf at a local course. We rented clubs and gave it a valiant try in a howling, but typical, Irish wind. But the greens were the worst of it, elevated and hard as cement, not your typical California course. There was no way for your beautiful shot to hold. We finished 18 holes, but I refuse to reveal our scores.

We toured the city of Cobh in County Cork and learned that the Titanic left from this last port after departing from Southampton, England. Also, from here three million people tragically emigrated from Ireland due to the potato famine in 1845-9. We drove the 120-mile Ring of Kerry to enjoy the scenery of lakes, castle ruins, beaches, glens, mountains, and ocean. The incomparable beauty of the nearly vertical Cliffs of Moher is the highlight of County Clare. They are 700 feet above the Atlantic and run for five miles along the coast.

From there we drove through the town of Limerick, where we all invented our own limericks and recited them on the bus. Mine was not original, except I inserted the name of our female guide.

"There once was a maid from Madras, who had a fine little ass. Not round and pink, as you might think, but had ears, a long tail, and ate grass." Merle created several original ones but, like many limericks, are not printable in mixed company.

At one hotel we were entertained when one of our party (Luray) got up in the middle of the night, looking in the dark for the restroom, but locking herself in the closet instead. She made a lot of commotion before Al let her out. We recreated this story and the limericks on the flight home.

Kurth Krause

Israel and Jordon

This may have been my favorite OAT trip. However, Osama Bin Laden was killed as we were en route to Jordon. So, the guide told us to be careful with our short walk from our hotel to a local restaurant because there could be some terrorists who might not look kindly on a pair of Americans. We did notice the restaurant guard carrying an Uzi. When we got back to the hotel, we learned that only nine of our fellow travelers had signed up for the Jordon extension. This made the tour even better.

We spent our first full day exploring the well-preserved Roman ruins in Amman and Jerash. I did not realize that the Romans under Pompeii had conquered and transformed these towns into beautiful, stately, prosperous cities before Christ. We were impressed by Hadrian's Arch, the remains of the Hippodrome where they still hold chariot races with people dressed as gladiators and Roman centurions, the 3,000-seat south theater, and the Forum with 56 pillars. We also admired the Temple of Hercules inside the Amman Citadel with two complete 30-foot pillars.

We had dinner in a Muslim home and learned some of their culture. The mother spoke little English, but her two daughters were proficient. Their father was divorced from their mother but lived upstairs with his new wife. The daughters, 27- and 29- years-old, were unmarried and living at home. Both were well-educated and professional. The younger daughter was engaged to be married. Her fiancé had to prove he could support her in their own home and had to give the family gold as an inverse dowry. Therefore, the Jordanian Muslims marry late to amass sufficient wealth as a prerequisite to marriage. We were surprised at their modern, Western dress, no burkas or significant coverings of their bodies or faces.

The highlight of Jordon and the main reason for adding it to our Israel tour was the UNESCO World Heritage Site of Petra.

But first we stopped in the north section of the Petra Archaeological Park to visit the site known as Little Petra. Like Petra itself, but much smaller, it displays 2,000-year-old buildings carved into the walls of the 1,480-foot-long sandstone canyon. Excavated in the mid-20th century, the carvings have been amazingly well preserved, even with excellent detailed art in some rooms and frescos in the ceiling. The high walls through the narrow canyon emitted little sunlight. There we witnessed workers setting up for a Jordanian wedding that night.

As one of the New Seven Wonders of the World, Petra itself took our breath away. It remained unknown to the Western world until 1812. It is believed to have been established in 312 BC. It was the capital of the nomad Nobataeans and a major regional trading hub with an estimated 20,000 inhabitants. It fell to the Romans in 106 AD. It is best known for its majestically preserved "Treasury" carved into the sandstone cliff. A massive theater is also remarkable. Several homes carved into the walls are prominent.

Crossing into Israel from Jordon was unexpected. The Israeli security displayed both friendliness and efficiency. They gave us the option of not stamping our passports. They explained that a passport stamped from Israel, could give us problems if we wanted to enter a Muslim country, or even Palestinian territory. So, we elected to just stamp a separate document, so that the passport would not indicate that we had entered Israel. We were then transferred from the Jordanian guide to an Israeli guide, a thirty-something woman, who, like all young Israelis, had served two years in the Israeli military. She was cordial and friendly, but her military training was apparent.

We had stimulating face-to-face contact with such a diverse group of people in Israel that it seemed like were not visiting such a tiny country, but many countries. We had dinner with an ultra-orthodox Hasidic Jew with his black curly braids dangling down the sides of his face and his black hat and robe. He explained his sole purpose is to be a scholar of the Torah and Talmud, which he studied daily, while his wife supported him. He aspired to follow all 613 commandments of the Torah (The Law).

We spent two hours with a Holocaust survivor, had lunch with a Bedouin family, met 1½ hours with an angry Palestinian, and had lunch with a Druze family just one day before their village was overrun by Lebanon terrorists. We spent two nights in a beautiful kibbutz overlooking the Sea of Galilee. The first night we had dinner with the kibbutz leader. He told us that when they first arrived from Russia, they were a communist kibbutz, but quickly converted to socialism. Then, when they realized their best workers were leaving, they became a capitalist kibbutz and greatly prospered ever since.

We went down the Golan Heights to board a boat to cross the biblical Sea of Galilee where Jesus performed his miracles. Fed by the Jordon River at the north, it is the lowest freshwater lake in the world, 700 feet below sea level and 33 miles in circumference. The Israeli captain was hospitable and played Christian hymns, including *How Great Thou Art* on the boat's loudspeaker as we crossed.

At the south of the lake, Galilee flows back into the Jordon, which then flows south through the West Bank and into the Dead Sea, at an elevation of 1,300 feet below sea level, the lowest land elevation on earth. It is also one of the saltiest bodies of water on earth at 34%, almost ten times as salty as the ocean. There we floated effortlessly on our backs—what an amazing feeling. We also witnessed adult baptisms with total immersion upstream in the Jordon.

We were anxious to visit Jerusalem. We first walked the Via Dolorosa in the Old City, the fourteen Stations of the Cross believed to be the exact route Jesus took bearing his cross to his crucifixion. It was solemn but rushed. Our guide explained we had to stay ahead of Palestinian protestors who had gathered at Lion's Gate because a 17-year-old Palestinian terrorist had been killed by the Israeli Army the previous day. Next, we found the 1,600-foot-long, 62-foot-high Wailing Wall, a part of the original Western Wall, the only remains of the biblical Second Temple of Jerusalem created by Herod the Great in 19 BC. The "Wailing Wall" is a western term to depict the Israelis mourning the destruction of their temple by the Romans in 70 AD. It is sacred to the Israelis who form lines (one for the men, another for women) to place their written prayers into crevices in the wall, as we did.

We traveled ten miles south of Jerusalem to Bethlehem for a day, but it was not as thrilling as I had hoped. Since Bethlehem was in Palestinian territory in the West Bank, we had to trade our Israeli guide for a Palestinian. We saw the Church of the Nativity, originally constructed in 339 AD to mark the place of Jesus' birth, as one of the holiest places in Christendom. The church has been a Christian pilgrimage from Jerusalem for 1,700 years. We walked down a hot, narrow passage under the church to an opening said to be the location of the manger of baby Jesus. Then we went out to Shepherd Field a few miles from Bethlehem, believed to be the location where the angels announced Jesus' birth to the shepherds. But the actual location was speculation.

We traveled three miles south of Bethlehem to visit a striking ancient palace, the Herodian. Here, Herod the Great built his palace fortress between 23 and 15 BC 2,500 feet above sea level. After exploring the top of the structure, we ventured down steep stairs into the gigantic cistern, built to house the water necessary to survive at the edge of the Judean desert. The size of this colossal creation amazed me.

We reentered Israel to visit Masada, the hilltop fortress under siege by the Roman Army in 73 AD, one of the last conflicts between the Israelis and the Roman Empire. Thousands of Roman soldiers and their slaves eventually stormed the sect of Jewish Zealots in Masada to put down the Jewish rebellion. But the 960 Sicarii rebels killed themselves, rather than be captured and enslaved.

OAT held our farewell dinner in modern Tel Aviv overlooking the beautiful Mediterranean before the long flight home. I would recommend that Israel be on the short list of any world traveler.

Prague and Bratislava

We toured Eastern Europe for the first time since the fall of the Soviet Union. Czechoslovakia had recently split into the Czech Republic and Slovakia. The beauty of Prague, the Czech Republic capital, impressed me. It is called the city of 100 spires. At night we would walk to the heart of the historic district, Old Town Square, to admire the Gothic churches, spires, and colorful baroque edifices. The medieval astronomical clock in the square center gave animated shows every hour. The Charles Bridge spans the Vltava River. Built in the ninth century, Prague Castle is particularly impressive. It is the largest castle in the world at 750,000 square feet, containing the Bohemian Crown Jewels. I was disappointed when our young guide told me that the population has been steadily turning from Christianity since the early 20th century. It is now one of the least religious countries in Europe at 20% of the population, Christianity being less than 12%. I thought that after they got rid of the oppression of communism, they would be returning to a strong Christian majority.

Bratislava, the capital of Slavia is only 45 miles from Vienna, Austria. Compared to glamorous Prague, it could be disappointing and mundane. But it turned out to be a fun city that we would not forget. On our way to the city, we made our own head gear out of balloons, under the tutelage of a member of our group who was a professional balloon artist. We had been invited to a mock wedding to experience their customs. After the ceremony at the church, we retrieved and donned our head gear and some bubble-blowing paraphernalia. We walked with the wedding party to the reception in a music hall, blowing bubbles along the way, to the delight of the children who began following our procession. By the time we reached the reception, we were all jacked up. They loved our crazy hats and invited us to dance with the wedding party—mostly polkas. We presented our balloon hats to the wedding guests and bubbles to the children. For us it was the highlight of Bratislava.

Peru and Galapagos

Our tour began at 11,000 feet in the Andes at Cuzco, Peru, the 13th century center of the Incan Empire. Sue and I had prepared for the altitude by spending a night before we left at 7,000 feet in Big Bear in the California mountains and brought altitude sickness pills. But it was not enough. Soon after we arrived, we started feeling ill. Our guide gave us a drink made with cocoa beans and had us lie down for two hours. Although we were concerned about getting high on cocoa beans, it worked, and we felt great. Sometimes local cures trump prescribed medication. Later we watched a shaman, a native Peruvian spiritual leader, get high smoking cocoa to enable his "altered state of consciousness" to interact with the spiritual world. The guide took us to a typical indigenous Peruvian Andes home: dirt floor with pet guinea pigs running around. (These pets also doubled as food for the native family.)

We climbed up to 12,000 feet altitude to the ruins of a citadel adjacent to and north of Cuzco called Saqsaywaman, an UNESCO World Heritage site. The Incas built it in the twelfth and thirteen centuries. It contains a giant plaza with three immense 20-foot high terrace walls built from huge stones remaining after decimation of the complex by the Spaniards. The 100- to 200-ton stones were carefully fit together without mortar, yet so tight I could not fit a single piece of paper between them, nor fit a pin in their joints. They have survived Peru's devastating earthquakes.

We visited the villages of the native Peruvian tribes in the Sacred Valley of the Incas at a 12,500-foot altitude to learn how the indigenous people traditionally weaved their bright-colored blankets, hats, and clothes. We loved the tribesmen displaying their colorfully adorned llamas and entertaining us with a one-man band. We saw some of the woven items offered to us when our train to "The Lost City of the Incas" made stops along the route.

Our train from Cuzco to Machu Picchu went down through the Andes in switchback fashion to compensate for the dramatic grade. Machu Picchu is less than 8,000-feet altitude and 50 miles northwest of Cuzco. We spent the night at the base of the mountain, then switchback-ascended in a bus to the UNESCO World Heritage Site the next morning.

This amazing ancient city on top of a mountain was constructed circa 1450 but abandoned by the Incas 100 years later when they were conquered by the Spaniards. It was rediscovered in 1911, when the overgrowth of the forest began to be cleared. Restoration continues today. It is now one of the New Seven

Wonders of the World. The ruins of nearly 200 buildings on terraces on two distinct levels surround the central square. Most impressive are the Temple of the Sun and the Room of the Three Windows. Another mountainous landscape, Huayna Picchu, rises less than a mile from the complex to 8,800 feet.

The setting was particularly breathtaking for me, due to my acrophobia. Two other women in our group were also afraid of heights. I dubbed us the "Sure-Footed California Wall Huggers," as our hands received insect bites from hanging on to every vegetation-covered wall as we navigated the scary complex. Two insane adventurers of our group, a couple from England, actually climbed up the worn, narrow, fragile, stone staircase to the top of Huayna Picchu. But they received many insect bites on their legs for their trouble. As we re-boarded our bus, we were challenged by two native boys that they could beat the bus down the mountain on foot. Indeed, they did by running straight down the treacherous slope, while the bus was negotiating a switchback route.

Then we were off to Quito, Ecuador for a flight to the Galapagos Islands, 600 miles due west on the equator. Since our group consisted of only 14 people, we were joined on the Galapagos boat by the Spanish ambassador to Equator and his pretty twenty-something wife. She became a handful for our poor guide. He instructed us as to how important it was to stay quiet on the well-marked path to not disturb the vast diversity of wildlife.

Our new boat was cheaply made, and minor pieces kept falling off. The rough weather made the trips between the islands uncomfortable with furniture inside the second deck staterooms bouncing off the walls.

In 1835, Charles Darwin surveyed these islands in his boat, *HMS Beagle*. In 1859, he wrote his famous book, *The Origin of the Species*. We spent seven days exploring eight of these amazing islands and their diverse and tame wildlife. There were so many marine iguanas of every color that we had to be careful not to step on them. Because one was required to only walk on the defined paths (except the ambassador's wife who would flit everywhere except on the paths), the animals had no fear. Many cannot be found elsewhere. Most of the islands were uninhabited. We approached within three feet of an albatross chick in its nest. The bright red, orange, and yellow Grapsus crab was easy to spot on San Cristóbal Island. We swam with the playful Galapagos Sea Lions and sunned ourselves next to them on the beaches. The Galapagos islands are dry, mostly hardened lava. Therefore, Darwin's finch may sit on your shoulder to get any water you may have. The blue-footed booby is spectacular with his bright blue feet and mating dancing skills. But most dramatic is the 900-pound Galapagos giant tortoise, who can live over 100 years.

The chilly 69-degree water temperature did not deter us from swimming with the sea creatures off the boat. The ambassador's wife braved it in her tiny bikini. But three of our seventy-something female passengers entertained us with a water ballet that displayed real expertise in the sport. The sea lions seemed to enjoy it as well.

Japan

We spent two weeks exploring Japan, one of Sue's favorite OAT trips, Although the Japanese are very nationalistic, discouraging citizenship for non-Japanese, they were outwardly quite friendly. But their demographics have been hurting the country because their birth rate is low, and their population is aging. As a result, racism and xenophobia are on the decline and more foreign nationals are now being accepted as citizens.

We noticed that the Japanese were well-dressed and well-groomed, but many wore face masks in Tokyo even though pollution did not appear to be a problem. We had lunch at the home of a gracious elderly couple. His trophies as a marathon runner adorned the room.

We spent two nights at a traditional Japanese guest house in the mountains of Hakone. We had to remove our shoes at the door, then don slippers and a yukata robe to enter. Furniture was sparse with a low table for dining on the floor. On the tatami-mat floor were traditional futons on which to sleep—a unique experience. We burned incense in the Shinto shrine on the shore of Lake Ashi. On the third morning, we boarded a cable car to climb up the mountainside. As we reached the apex, we received a spectacular view of iconic Mount Fuji as it penetrated the bank of clouds usually hiding this perfectly shaped volcano. We took a 200-mph bullet train, one of the fastest in the world, to Kanazawa. It was right on time and accelerated smoothly—very impressive.

Our final stop was the beautiful city of Kyoto. We timed this perfectly as it was the peak of cherry blossom time. The petals fell all around us as we walked through a sand and rock garden. It was enchanting. The next day as we headed for the Osaka airport, the rain brought virtually all the blossoms down.

Central America – the Mayans

Our guide greeted us at the San Salvador airport in El Salvador. His nickname was Rambo, which we learned to be fitting. He was a mercenary. He had set up the jungle setting for the *Survivor* TV show. Here, we visited our first Mayan dwelling, Joya de Cerein, which like Pompeii had been buried under 20 feet of volcanic ash for 1,500 years. The next day we drove to

Honduras to explore the ancient city of Copan, another UNESCO World Heritage Site. It occupies 37 acres, initially built by a Mayan king in 426 AD and modified by successive kings for the next 400 years. At the central plaza is an acropolis surrounded by temples. The Temple of the Hieroglyphic Stairway is a pyramid of 2,000 glyphs carved into 63 ascending steps. The city is known for the 166 stelae images (tall, sculptured monuments to prominent Mayans), mostly located along the processional way of the central plaza.

As we crossed the border into Guatemala, Rambo had to use his influence with his guns displayed, giving small bribes to the border guards. We cruised the deepest lake in Central America, Lake Atitlan, and enjoyed its beauty. Then we drove on to another UNESCO World Heritage Site, Antigua, to explore the La Merced ruins. After visiting Guatemala City, we traversed the rainforest to Tikal, another 1,800-year-old Mayan UNESCO World Heritage Site. It boasts of over 1,000 buildings (many not yet excavated) covering 23 square miles, including the giant ceremonial Lost World Pyramid and the 240-foot high Temple of the Grand Jaguar. One female in our group was quite an athlete. She ran up the narrow stairs to the top, but none of us dared to follow.

We traveled to the site of Cahul Pech in Belize as our last stop. It too has a central acropolis, surrounded by 34 structures. It was built as early as 1200 BC. Its tallest temple is 80 feet. Excavation began in 1988. Belize is a fun place with restaurants along the beach on sand stilts and good snorkeling along the reefs.

Kenya Safari

This was one of our best land tours, although it was not guided by OAT. Instead Abercrombie and Kent were hired by the now defunct cruise line, Renaissance. They chartered a modified 737 for 114 passengers (the capacity of their ship), which took us to Kenya, the Seychelles, and Egypt in 1997. Abercrombie and Kent did not disappoint.

I anticipated the highlight would be our small cruise ship sailing through the beautiful Seychelles in the middle of the Indian Ocean. Indeed, we did enjoy the Seychelles. We hired a fishing boat to take us out to the middle of the Indian Ocean where Sue caught a beautiful Dorado (Mahi Mahi), but the fishing boat captain stole her fish as he dropped us off at our ship.

I thought the safari in Kenya would not be as exciting, looking through field glasses trying to spot the animals while riding in a Range Rover; then having to spend several nights in a crummy tent. I could not have been more wrong.

In Nairobi, we had dinner at the Carnivore Restaurant where they served every type of game on a long skewer: hartebeest, crocodile, ostrich, ox testicles. Outside were wart hogs running around and several giraffes who showed you how long their tongues were.

The next day we boarded a small single-engine prop plane to reach the camp in the Maasai Mara Reserve of Kenya. The pilot had to buzz the landing strip one time to scare the baboons off the runway for us to land safely. We settled into our spacious tent with twin beds and nightstands, a dressing area, and three separate partitions for a shower, sink, and commode, all with hot water heated by firewood. I had been in hotel rooms less comfortable. As soon as we were settled, we were off on our first safari with one other couple and our guide/driver. Not far outside the camp, we encountered a pride of lions who had just killed a zebra. They were busy eating, so they seemed to have no interest in us even though we were only twenty feet away. The females kill the prey; then the male eats first, followed by the females and then the cubs. What a fascinating spectacle.

We returned to our luxurious tent to get ready for dinner. We had to tie the zipper to the tent closed or the monkeys could get in. A tall electrified barbed-wire fence enclosed the camp to protect us from the lions, but the monkeys easily climbed the surrounding trees to drop in. We first went to the outdoor bar where we could order top-shelf liquor, then to a gourmet outdoor meal. Afterward three men from the Maasai tribes entertained us by dancing and jumping to music. These guys were at least six feet six inches tall and they could really jump. We returned to our tent to find hot-water bottles in our beds. Even though we were on the equator, the daytime temperature was in the 70s and it got chilly at night. That night we heard the roar of the lions and the loud screech of eastern hyraxes (large rodent-looking creatures related to the elephant).

Each day we went on two safari drives, which were amazing. We passed 15-20 giraffes walking single file almost 100 yards apart. When we came back, they were in a large circle, facing outward, apparently looking out for their carnivorous enemies. We illegally crossed into the Tanzania Serengeti to see two male lions who had brought down a water buffalo. One was still eating, while the other lay asleep on his back, paws up like a kitten. We saw the vicious hyenas chase the crazy herd of wildebeest until they caught one and ate it. The many types of antelope were highlighted by the graceful impalas leaping so high one would think there was no gravity. We ventured out on one drive where the guide stopped 25 feet from a small herd of elephants eating grass on both sides of the dirt road. Suddenly, one of the big bull elephants decided he did not like us there. He raised his head, fanned out his ears, let out a load trumpet, and started marching toward us. Our guide immediately backed up, turned around, and quickly drove away, explaining that elephants forewarned a charge exactly as the bull did. We stopped on the way back to see a cheetah resting, perhaps after a 60 mile-per-hour run.

We drove to the bank of the Mara River where 1.3 million wildebeest cross every spring to get to the grasslands. Many of their carcasses were lying along the banks or in the river where they had drowned. Wildebeests are quite stupid and easy prey. Buzzards were plentiful, waiting for a carnivore to rip open wildebeest bodies because the buzzards are unable to do so. In the water were the extremely dangerous hippos and crocodiles. We also saw some water buffalo but did not see the rare black rhino. They are endangered due to poaching.

We arouse early to take a hot air balloon ride over the plain. I was apprehensive about the height until I got into the basket and found the side wall was as high as my armpit. The ride was unexpectedly peaceful as we floated over the Maasai villages and the animals. When we came down the guides presented us with a champagne breakfast at our landing spot. It was quite a treat.

We visited a tribe's small village, enclosed by rough bramble bushes to keep the lions out. Approximately 30 women stood in a semi-circle and sang to entertain us. Many had their earlobes stretched and pierced, some adorned with beaded ornaments. Afterward we gave them gifts, mostly red garments because the Maasai were known to love red. Then we bought their carvings and woven items for mementos. They were happy to get our money. Finally, we were invited into the chief's three-room mud hut. He slept in one room, his wife and children in another, and the tribe's cow in a third. Their standard meal comes from a mixture of cow's milk and blood drained from an opening in the cow's ankle. Their stained teeth revealed their diet. On another day we witnessed an election where the members of many tribes lined up behind the official that they wish to elect. We were sorry to leave this interesting adventure into the Maasai Mara. We then flew the short flight back to Nairobi, where we boarded the chartered 737 for the 1,000-mile flight to the Seychelles.

Egypt

After the seven-day cruise around the beautiful Seychelle Islands with their magnificent palm trees and giant granite rocks, we again boarded the charter flight to Egypt. Three weeks earlier, a terrorist band had murdered two busloads of tourists, mostly Germans and Swiss, with the objective of destroying Egyptian tourism. As a result, 45 of our passengers elected to forgo Egypt, proceeding directly back to the United States because they were afraid. So, after the 737 dropped us off at Luxor, it flew them back. Normally Luxor is teaming with tourists, but we 69 were alone and had Luxor to ourselves. We had two guides assigned to our group, both Egyptologists, who taught us well.

Our accommodations were bungalows, which had armed guards patrolling all night to protect us. We rode our bus to the bazaar, and, after shopping late, the bus returned the two of us back to our hotel compound. A jeep with four armed guards followed our bus. We felt completely safe.

We spent the morning at the acclaimed outdoor Karnak Temple. The building of the complex began around 2000 BC and continued until 30 BC. Only the Giza Pyramids are visited by more tourists in Egypt. Normally over 10,000 people would be here daily. But, because of the terrorist attack, the only people here other than us were a few school children. It is estimated that 30 pharaohs had a hand in Temple design and construction. Inside the walls, the Hypostyle Hall occupies 50,000 square feet with 134 massive columns, including 12 that are 65 feet tall with a diameter of almost ten feet. Across the top are architraves weighing 70 tons.

Several theories exist as to how these slabs were placed on top, including that the complex was filled with sand, the slabs dragged up to their positions, then the sand excavated. One temple has a 95-foot-high obelisk weighing over 700 tons. Hieroglyphs are present throughout on the pillars, the friezes, and the monuments. Several movies feature Karnak as a backdrop.

It was disheartening to visit the Nile River in Luxor. Normally over 100 double-decker river boats would motor up and down the Nile between Luxor and Aswan. All these boats were docked four across and their crews laid off. We took a felucca up the river a short distance, enjoyed tea and cake, then back to Luxor, just to get a feel for these old wooden sailboats and to generate some revenue for the owners.

We toured the Valley of the Kings on the west bank of the Nile, then the Valley of the Queens opposite the ancient city of Thebes. We were permitted to view Nefertari's Tomb. She was the favorite wife of Ramses II and her tomb is also called the Sistine Chapel of Ancient Egypt. Usually it is almost impossible to see because they only allowed 125 people per day, but since we were the only tourists—no problem. Although the tomb, like all the other known tombs, had been looted, the wall paintings were amazing, including depicting the exquisite features of the ancient queen. The ceiling of the antechamber represented the heavens. The paintings had just been restored and it looked like the artist had just taken a break from his work. The restoration by the Egyptian Antiquities Organization was financed by the Getty Foundation and completed in 1992.

We ventured to the open Hatshepsut Temple, where the terrorist murders had occurred just three weeks earlier. There were armed guards stationed in sniper position all around the elevated perimeter. Inside were young Egyptians with a logo on tee shirts that indicated "Down with Terrorism." They gave one to Sue. CNN covered their demonstration. Since we were the only tourists present, they interviewed us live on CNN.

We chose to take an early-morning flight to Cairo to see the pyramids and the Great Sphinx, another UNESCO World Heritage Site. They are in Giza at the edge of the western desert just outside the sprawling city of Cairo. The Great Pyramid, constructed 2580-2560 BC, is the oldest of the Ancient Wonders of the World and the only one still in existence. It is 481 feet tall. Several theories attempt to explain how these tombs for ancient pharaohs were built. Most are based on transporting these giant stones from a quarry on river barges, then dragged up over a sand ramp to be placed precisely. But the grade of the ramp, if linear, would place it out into the river. Another is that the ramp wound through the center of the pyramid.

The Great Sphinx is 240 feet long and 66 feet high, built around 2500 BC for the pharaoh Khafre. It was carved into the bedrock of a plateau on the west bank of the Nile within easy walking distance of the Great Pyramid. It is widely considered the world's most wonderful statue. One of our Egyptologist guides published a book that theorized that originally there must have been two Sphinxes, but one was destroyed and eroded away.

The final night in Luxor, the guides put on an authentic Egyptian performance including the Whirling Dervishes. Before we returned to Luxor, we had a cartouche made with Sue's name spelled out in ancient Egyptian symbols. Then we boarded the Charter 737 home on a trip we will never forget.

Highlights of Cruising

Although our cruises were not as memorable as the land tours, they offered a great deal of pleasure, if not as much adventure. Obviously, we enjoyed cruising, or we would not have tried it 41 times. The biggest advantage is seeing wonderful destinations, if only for relatively short times, by not having to pack and unpack throughout the cruise and being pampered. Initially, our favorite set of cruise ships was the Renaissance line. It began with eight small ships: four with 100 passengers, four with 114. They were more casual with open seating for all meals and no midnight buffets, which suited us. The cabins were ample, and all were suites with balconies. The food was excellent. It was easy to meet people and easier to navigate the shorter hallways. Best of all, the prices were not too high for what they offered, although somewhat higher than land tours. Eventually Renaissance sold off their small ships, replacing them with eight identical midsize vessels with a capacity of 684 passengers. They were beautiful in design and we loved them as much as the small ships. But they declared bankruptcy and went out of business on 25 September 2001. Azamara bought three of their ships, Oceania bought four, and Princess bought one.

    Our next set of favorite cruises was the Celebrity line. We sailed on several classes of their ships often enough that we received perks, such as access to private rooms for breakfast and cocktail parties. Since they were owned by Royal Caribbean, we also received perks the few times we sailed with them. Our current favorite is the Regent Seven Seas line, with which we also receive minor perks as frequent guests. We did sail other ships, including Windstar, Oceania, Princess, and Crystal. But they never made it into our list of favorites, even though we enjoyed them. With some of these cruises we were joined by friends, as many as three other couples. We also made new friends, six of whom we have since visited in other parts of the country.

Some of the most memorable cruises usually involved some great destinations. A Baltic cruise included three days in St. Petersburg, the cultural and historic heart of Russia. Mike, Merle, Don, and Vanda from our country club got together with us to hire a private guide and a driver. This turned out to be a great choice. The guide got us into the Heritage Museum when the crowds were down, so we could see almost everything in less than a day. Housed in six buildings, it is the second largest museum in the world next to the Louvre and has the largest collection of art in the world. Our guide also got us into the wine cellar where Rasputin, the mystic and favored friend of the Russian Emperor Nicholas II, was assassinated.

We toured the czar's winter palace and the massive open city square in front. This is where Czar Alexander II was shot in 1879, and the Bolshevik Revolution started in 1917. We toured the palaces of Alexander I and Catherine the Great. Our final visit was St. Basil's Cathedral, within walking distance of our ship. It did not look striking from the outside, but its interior was amazing with malachite green pillars and impressive artwork.

Our first cruise to French Polynesia was on the Windsong, a four-mast sailing ship with only 74 cabins. We could not ask for a more enjoyable cruise. We visited what for me were the two most beautiful islands in the world: Bora Bora and Moorea. The ship had fun beach toys such as jet skis and snorkeling for the guests. We "swam with the sharks" with the guide feeding them fish just a few feet from our bodies. We also had manta rays brush our ankles while wading off one of the islands. After the eight-day cruise, we navigated a hill next to the dock to reach a nice restaurant overlooking the Tahiti harbor. It was so sad to see our beautiful ship sail away without us and with new passengers. We liked it so much that we took two more cruises to French Polynesia during the next 20 years.

One of my favorite cruise ports in the world is Rio de Janeiro. The first time there we arrived for Carnival, an amazing celebration throughout Rio. Young adults were sleeping in the parks after a long night of celebration; two million people were in the streets. During the day, music appeared throughout the city. We bought Carnival tickets for the first night of the two-day parade by samba schools traversing down the Sambadrome, called the biggest show on earth. Fourteen samba schools prepare for a year with original costumes, music, dance, and floats to compete for $1,000,000 to the winner. Each school begins with fireworks, their music blasting through loudspeakers as 2,000 costume-clad choreographed dancers began their 85-minute, half-mile trek in front of 90,000 spectators for "The Greatest Party on the Planet." Not all were completely clad since the top tiers on their ten gigantic floats displayed topless dancers. Since it started at 9 PM, we only stayed until 2 AM to see three of the schools perform. I understood why so many young people were sleeping on the grass during the day.

But Rio has more to offer than Carnival. The Ipanema and Copacabana Beaches are world renown. The city views from Sugar Loaf Mountain and Christ the Redeemer are spectacular with houses in valleys running between the many city hills. Rio is also famous for hang gliding off the cliffs and for some of the world-famous jewelry stores, where one can stay safe among the petty thieves by being assigned a driver from these stores. We went back to Rio twice more to take in their adventures.

Istanbul, Turkey became one of our favorite cruise ports. The merchants in 4,000 shops in the Grand Bazaar were entertaining, selling their distinctive carpets, leather clothes, and jewelry. We toured the Blue Mosque, the Topkapi Palace, and the Great Mosque. The Bosporus, the strait that bisects Turkey, also separates Europe from Asia. We took a ferry to the quaint Princes' Islands, where only horse and buggy transportation is allowed.

We were a bit adventurous in our cruise around Cape Horn. We and Merle and Mike started in Santiago Chile, but quickly cruised for Tierra del Fuego and the northern boundary of the Drake passage where the Pacific and Atlantic meet. This passage is usually rough sailing as the waters around Cape Horn are particularly hazardous and known as one of the major challenges in yachting. But we were fortunate to be able to get through the narrow Strait of Magellan. At one of our stops, Sue took a two-hour bus ride to walk along with millions of penguins. We were supposed to cruise to the Falklands, but the Captain decided the seas were too rough.

Taking a Regent cruise ship through the mighty Amazon River in Brazil and Columbia was unforgettable. Although the Nile is slightly longer (longest in the world), the volume of water is larger than the Mississippi, the Yangtze, and the Nile combined. In the rainy season it discharges 12 million cubic feet per second into the Atlantic Ocean. Although several rivers from the mountains on the Western side of South America feed the Amazon, ultimately two major rivers, Rio Negro and Solimoes meet at the largest city on the Amazon: Manaus. These two rivers of different color and density join, but do not mix, displaying a dramatic view of the separate rivers.

The Amazon rainforest spans over nine countries and is home to 30% of the world's animals and 40,000 plant species. It produces 20% of the world's oxygen. The average annual precipitation is nine feet, spiking to 35 feet in some areas. It is home to the most vivid pink dolphins and the voracious piranha, which we caught with red meat on our hooks. The black caiman looks like a large crocodile, but the green anaconda is equally frightening, over 15 feet long. Less visually fearsome, but deadly, are the poison dart frogs which we met in Costa Rica.

Other great cruise stops for us included Dubai, Mumbai, Cape Town, Ho Chi Minh City, Taipei, Buenos Aires, Angkor Wat, Easter Island, the Greek islands, Manila, Crete, Malta, Sicily, the Faroe Islands, Corsica, Cyprus, Gibraltar, Iceland, Dubrovnik, and Alaska. Our cruises through the Panama Canal and the St. Lawrence Seaway were also interesting.

My least favorite cruise port became Cabo San Lucas, but only because of an excursion. We took a whale-watching boat and made the mistake of accepting a can of Coke. When we got back to the ship, I became so sick that they had to quarantine us in our cabin for three days until the symptoms ended.

I left copies of my book, *My 36 Years in Space*, in the libraries of Regent and Celebrity ships and received wonderful comments on these. Some readers, including a Regent captain, bought their own copies after reading the ship's copy. I wish I had donated copies to all the ship libraries. I may do the same with this book.

We enjoyed many cruises to the Caribbean islands. They offered the best snorkeling, particularly in the Cayman Islands, Belize, Cozumel, Antigua, and the Virgin Islands. Our favorite is Buck Island adjacent to St. Croix, which John Kennedy named a national monument after he snorkeled there. But in my opinion, the many islands here do not compare to the beauty of French Polynesia or the Hawaiian Islands.

Domestic Travel

I do not want to minimize the great experiences we enjoyed traveling with our friends and family throughout North America. We visited friends in Idaho. We loved the golf course at the Coeur D' Alene Resort where Sue and I were awarded a certificate for parring their famous island green. We also had a great time with our friends, Bob and Ann, playing in their couples' member-guest tournament on three wonderful courses in Austin, Texas, including the Ben Crenshaw-designed Barton Creek.

We rented a car with Mike and Merle in Spokane Washington to drive to the beautiful sites in Washington, Montana, and Alberta Canada. We also played at the Banff Springs Golf Course where we stopped to watch a pair of gigantic elk observing us from right off the third green. We spent the night at the Lake Louise Fairmont Hotel to take in the surrounding beauty. We drove through a rainy Glacier National Park in Montana for our final destination through the Northwest.

Mike and Merle also accompanied us on a two-week drive through the many wonderful national parks in Utah and Arizona. We first stopped in Sedona to take in the splendor of its colorful bluffs once again. Next, we drove to the Monument Valley Navajo Tribal Park, where Sue sketched the ninety-year-old matriarch in her tent. The hoodoos in Bryce Canyon National Park were the highlight. But the sheer cliffs of Zion were a close second. We also enjoyed Arches National Park, Canyonlands, Capital Reef, the Bridges National Monument, and the Grand Staircase National Monument. There was something for everyone.

We celebrated our special wedding anniversaries with our family. For our 45th, we bought a package at the Los Caballeros dude ranch in Wickenburg, Arizona for the ten of us, playing golf, riding horses, getting massages, playing tennis, and swimming. An astronomer gave us a telescope show, and we went on a hayride, listening to a guitar-playing singer for the nighttime entertainment. For our 50th anniversary we rented three villas for our three families in Wailea, Maui. There we played golf, surfed, snorkeled, road bikes down from the Haleakala Crater, and attended a luau. These family reunions were unforgettable.

Sue and I also had great Hawaiian golfing vacations on our own in Oahu, Kauai, Maui, and the Big Island. Especially memorable were the beauty of Hanalei Bay, the rough road to Hana, the helicopter ride over the Kilauea lava flow, the six great golf courses in Wailea, Kapalua, and Makena, and the snorkeling in the semi-submerged Molokini crater.

We took an escorted 24-person Tauck tour through the Bourbon Trail. It began at Churchill Downs in Kentucky, listening to anecdotes from a retired jockey as we watched the horses on the track. We visited the Kentucky bourbon distilleries along the Bourbon Trail on our way through the Smokey Mountains. We spent the night in the famous Biltmore Hotel in Asheville, North Carolina. We ended up enjoying the Grand Ole Opry in Nashville and were treated to a private serenade by a Nashville song writer.

We visited our son's family in Alexandria Virginia several times. We never tire of touring our nation's capital: The National Mall, the Smithsonian Air and Space Museum, the Lincoln Memorial, the war memorials, the Washington Monument, and the Air Force Memorial. No American should miss these great sites.

Of course, we found New York City a great place to visit. We saw the World Trade Center Twin Towers before their destruction and visited the 9/11 Memorial afterward. Little Italy, Chinatown, Central Park, Rockefeller Center, Radio City Music Hall, and Times Square are all worth a visit. For me, the best are the Broadway musicals. Somehow, they seem more exciting in New York than Southern California.

Our cruises through Alaska were also unforgettable. We loved observing the caving in Glacier Bay, taking a helicopter ride to the Mendenhall Glacier, walking on it, and watching our family zipline at Icy Strait Point. Enjoying a beer at a bar in little towns of Juneau, Skagway, and Ketchikan was fun. Denali is spectacular.

We also enjoyed a driving trip with Mike and Merle through New Mexico. We did miss some important sites. High winds prevented the launching of the hot air balloons in Albuquerque. We were not permitted to visit the famous Taos Pueblo due to a tribal funeral. We bypassed the wonderful Carlsbad Cavern because we had taken our children there in 1975. Still we had a good trip, learning about and seeing the exhibits at the Indian Pueblo Culture Center, taking the tramway to Sandia Peak in Albuquerque, and dining at Vernon's Speakeasy. We found this place surreptitiously, obtaining the password from a departing guest. A bouncer opened the viewing slot in a large black wooden door under a red light to receive our password, then welcomed us while holding a baseball bat. The place was dark, prices unexpectedly expensive, and the epitome of a prohibition speakeasy of the past. I inferred from the magazines in the lobby that this speakeasy may be peddling marijuana.

Travel Recommendations

It is obvious by the space I have devoted to this chapter that travel has been an important part of our lives after our children had left the nest. Many were expensive, but worth it. Our memories are forever. While we found domestic travel stimulating, I highly recommend world travel because it is true that travel broadens your horizon. Learning about other people and destinations all over the world is not only educational, but entertaining. Traveling with friends can add enjoyment to the trip but makes it harder to meet new people.

It pays to shop around for pricing, especially cruises and airlines, not so much for guided tours. We have realized significant savings by going through consolidators, who buy up cruise cabin bookings and business class air fares at low prices and resell them to the public. Once I booked a business class reservation to Europe with a consolidator for $2,650 each, but when I repeatedly looked for the credit card charge, it was not there. I checked the United Airlines reservation, which showed our booking. So, I saved the name and phone number of the consolidator. When we tried to check in for the flight, we were told the reservation had not been paid but was still open. I reluctantly agreed to pay at the counter, thinking we would now have to pay full price of $3,700 each. But United charged us only $1,680 each, the price they charged the consolidator.

Timing can also make a big difference in price. I highly recommend business class for long flights. We will never fly coach overseas again because it is too hard on us both physically and mentally. I cannot sleep in coach, while business class offers a full flat bed for sleeping. Also, the business class airport lounge offers comfort, food, and drink while waiting for boarding. Once, when we flew to Dubai on Emirates, we enjoyed the special service in their first-class lounge because they did not have a separate lounge for business class at LAX. And after the flight back, a chauffeur greeted our arrival and drove us to our home in a limousine. Other benefits of business class include bypassing the coach security line, boarding early, and deplaning early. I suggest considering spending the $85 for the Transportation Security Agency's PreCheck card to bypass the security lines for domestic travel if you plan to travel more than once per year.

I always enjoyed planning for a trip. The anticipation and preparation extended the duration of the enjoyment of the trip itself. But I was always careful not to expect more than the trip offered. Perhaps this is why I was never disappointed. Returning home has usually been a downer, especially if jet lag is involved. I found it took me one day to recover for every hour of time difference.

If you enjoy the good life on a cruise, I recommend avoiding the low-cost fares offered by cruise lines like Carnival. In addition to the booking fare, add-ons like gratuities, beverages (especially alcoholic), snacks between meals, airfare, and excursions can pile up. Although it was the most expensive line, we liked Regent because it included business class airfare, gratuities, all beverages, and excursions in addition to great service.

I never bought trip insurance, which can be more than 10% of the total cost. Insurers make exorbitant profits on these policies. (See chapter on insurance.) However, occasionally I have purchased catastrophic medical insurance for foreign travel, which is a great deal cheaper ($200-400). My bridge partner broke her femur in Cambodia, and it cost her more than $30,000 to be medevacked to Bangkok for surgery, hospitalization, and medevacked home. We did have to cancel a $40,000 cruise for health reasons once, but I cancelled early enough that it only cost me 10%, which was less than the insurance premium.

15. RELIGION – NEVER TOO LATE

It took me over 60 years to "get it." I was raised an Evangelic United Brethren in suburban Milwaukee. Our family attended church irregularly, perhaps once per month. When I was 12, I started catechism training, but I felt like a hypocrite. What little reading of the Bible was forced on me did not resonate. I was not an atheist; I did believe in God, but I had many doubts about both the old and new testaments. I wanted to openly admit these doubts and refuse confirmation, but I did not want to embarrass my parents and grandparents, so I went through the motions. I wondered if any of the others in my confirmation class felt the same.

My paternal grandparents were much more devout than my parents. My grandmother was raised a Catholic and converted to Lutheranism when she married my grandfather. They attended church regularly and perhaps tithed. They read the Bible regularly (my parents did not) and had many religious books on their bookshelves.

My teenage years were no different. I continued to attend Sunday school and church irregularly. I do not remember discussing religion with my friends. I was mixed up and probably felt a little guilty that I had not accepted Christ. But I could not even get past *Genesis*. As I learned more about science and the dating of the evolution of the earth, the solar system, and the universe, the facts became irreconcilable with the Bible. I did not read much of the Bible and never really learned the history or the basic beliefs, including the Trinity, that Jesus died so that my sins would be forgiven, enabling me to enjoy an afterlife in heaven. But I always wondered.

In college, I continued to attend a Lutheran Church on occasion, not more than once per month. But as I learned more science, as I majored in math and physics, I easily dismissed much of *Genesis* as being the erroneous writings of early uneducated man. I never believed they were the word of God, or even inspired by God. But I was certainly not a religious scholar, having read only small portions of the Bible. Still, I believed in God and was aware of my real desire to seek the truth.

In graduate school, my church attendance dropped off even more as my fiancée, Sue, was away interning at various hospitals to fulfill her occupational therapy requirements. She was a stronger influence in attending church more regularly. After we were married and moved from Milwaukee to Boston to Houston, we attended several churches of different Protestant denominations, but neither of us was truly devoted to our faith and continued to search and wane. We did have our babies baptized in Milwaukee and Boston, respectively, but I cannot say we were bringing them up to be devout Christians.

It was no different when we moved to California in 1975. We did not join any church and became a family that rarely attended except Christmas and Easter. When Scott was of the age to study catechism, the commitment at the nearest Protestant church seemed beyond what I was ready to undertake, and we decided not to send him there. He was a very bright boy, quite mature, and I wanted him to learn about all religions before making a commitment. To my surprise he began attending the evening youth services at the Crystal Cathedral in Garden Grove with his friends. By age 13, Scott was totally immersed in Christian teachings, and struggled with his own commitment emotionally for many months. I was concerned about his obvious emotional struggle and wondered whether there was something "cultist" about his transformation at such an impressionable age. I went with him to one of the services, satisfied myself that there was nothing emotionally unhealthy with the environment, and accepted his commitment. Ultimately, he totally accepted Christ as his Savior and devoured the Bible. He started taking Sheryl to the services as well, and she became a Christian. He wanted Sue and me to do so as well, but I told him of my reservations. I remember telling him that I thought the reason the poor and downtrodden were so accepting of Christ unconditionally was that it gave them hope for a good afterlife they might otherwise never have. I said, "In my opinion the Hispanic Catholics used Christianity as a crutch. I believe that each of us has to make the best of this life on our own, and not expect God to fix our problems." For me, someone asking me to accept on faith was asking me to ignore the facts, intellect, logic, and reason that God had given me. Scott was clearly unhappy with this.

After Scott and Sheryl were both in college, Sue started attending church more regularly. Sheryl was married in the beautiful St. Andrews sanctuary in 1991. Soon afterwards Sue started attending St. Andrews regularly. She joined the Church in 1997 and persuaded me to attend more often. This resurrected my thirst for the truth. But there no overnight epiphany appeared.

I began attending other opportunities offered by St. Andrews. A writing class caught my eye. After I retired in 1999, I wanted to write a memoir of my personal career and experiences with the US space programs. I enjoyed the class, but being unaccustomed to praying within a group, felt a bit uncomfortable at first. Several months later, the group leader, Jeanie Ardell, suggested that Sue and I attend the St. Andrews couples' retreat that spring. I was inspired by the three-day retreat in the secluded southern California mountains. I became emotional at the final service, filled with praise songs and communion. I decided that perhaps, for the first time, the Holy Spirit had entered me. We attended the retreat almost every year for the next ten years.

I went home and began seeking the truth in earnest. One of the pastors, Lydia Sarandan, suggested a book, *The Case for Christ*, by Lee Strobel. I bought it and found it to be exactly what I had been seeking. Strobel was an agnostic journalist who was looking for a story by personally investigating history, logic, and facts to draw conclusions on whether Christ was indeed the son of God, had been crucified to save our sins, and was resurrected. Strobel became a Christian. Every argument hit home. I began accepting Christ as my savior. (Strobel's other book, *The Case for Faith*, I found disappointing, but maybe I was expecting too much.)

Next, Sue and I signed up for the two-year class, The Bethel Series. For the first time, I read the entire Bible, doing the homework assignments "religiously." It strengthened my faith, although there were still many passages in the Old Testament I could not accept. Our leader told us that details did not matter. All that was important from the Bible was to teach us how to live well and die well. This made a lot of sense to me.

I continued to read to try to reconcile conflicts between the Bible and science and my own concerns. One of the church members suggested Hugh Ross's *The Genesis Question.* Ross has doctorates in astronomy and physics as well as being a theologian and minister. He offers theories, by which many of the Bible's literal interpretations could be possible within the realm of physics, as we know it. Of course I've read many of the popular books, such as *The Purpose Driven Life,* by Rick Warren, *Evidence That Demands a Verdict,* by Josh McDowell, and many others, including those used by our covenant group, but they have not begun to provide as much meaning for me as Strobel and Ross. Not all my readings are pro-Christian. An atheist recommended *The Bible Unearthed,* by a Jewish archaeologist and a Jewish historian, which was very educational.

I reconciled my technical education with the Bible. I do believe that God created the universe but did so 14 billion years ago with the Big Bang. I believe God created humanity in his own image 200,000 years ago, not 4,000 years. I still believe the Old Testament has several flaws, written by imperfect humans, although inspired by God. I have accepted the New Testament, including the miracles attributed to Jesus. I do have trouble accepting *Revelations* because I do not understand it. I still have difficulty accepting that God will answer our prayers. I do not believe it is right to ask God for things to happen, other than to pray for healing. "Thy will, not my will, be done."

It is my opinion that Judas betrayed Jesus because it was part of God's plan for Jesus to die for our sins, then rise on Easter, and ascend to heaven 40 days later. I still have not accepted that Christ will return to earth again. I believe it is imperative that we believe in the Trinity to be accepted into heaven. I also believe that the problems in our lives are there to determine how well we deal with them, and we are judged accordingly. I now am at peace with the knowledge that someday my earthly life will end. I hope I leave a legacy that will please God.

I joined St. Andrews in 2003 and was happy to profess my acceptance of Jesus Christ. I still have misgivings about Old Testament Bible passages. Why did God not allow Moses to enter the promised land after all his godly deeds? Why did God have to kill the innocent firstborn sons of the Egyptians? My God could not advocate genocide of the Canaanites but would rather win them over to His real religion. He would not strike dead the poor man who tried to steady the Arc of the Covenant on the cart as David brought it back to Jerusalem. The conflicts of *Genesis*' chronology with scientific facts remains troubling. But these discrepancies, created by undereducated, often unknown authors are not at odds with "how to live and die well."

16. HAPPINESS IS A CHOICE

I have learned that people can *choose* whether to be content, happy, even filled with joy–or not. I had often heard that money does not buy happiness, but never quite believed it until later in life. There were many times when I, as a child, was quite happy:

- Coming home from school and listening to popular songs on the radio or the music of big bands on my dad's Victrola,
- Lying on the grass on a pleasant, summer day in Wisconsin, looking at cloud formations,
- Thinking of the pretty girl who smiled at me in class,
- Catching fish at Altoona Dam
- Going to a lake and staying in a cabin on a family vacation.
- Getting excused from school to watch the opening day game of the Milwaukee Braves

Sure, sometimes I was sad, depressed, and/or envious. Most of these times were brief due to short-term adverse relationships with other kids, but others were due to my family not able to afford things that other families could. Most of my friends were from families like mine, economically lower middle class.

But others were quite privileged with expensive new cars, large homes, month-long Florida vacations in January, nice new clothes, and discretionary money in their pockets.

When I attended college and then entered the workplace, I saw many other instances of a higher standard of living and aspired to it. I was quite content, doing much better than my father, but wanted more of the good life, which I thought could be achieved by earning more money: luxury cars, country club membership, traveling around the world, ocean cruises, and larger homes in upscale neighborhoods. I can't say I was ever really unhappy without these things, but I did think they would make me happier, especially if I could treat my wife to these things, some of which she had as a child.

Over the years, we acquired each of these things. While they did bring pleasure, they did not bring long-term happiness per se. Real happiness came from my wife and kids and from professional achievement, not from our possessions. Moreover, many famous, rich people were clearly unhappy, despite their fame and fortune. I also observed that some people in poverty seemed quite happy. I particularly noticed that, in general, Christians seemed happier than non-believers.

Several books helped me to solve this quandary, ranging from early publications like Norman Vincent Peale's *Power of Positive Thinking* to more modern *Easier Than You Think* by Richard Carlson. Their messages ring true for me. The wisdom of this in one form or another is, of course, timeless. "Do unto others as you would have them do onto you," has been around forever. It just took me a while to buy into it. Doing things *for* others makes one feel good. Doing things *to* others spoils that contentment. Anger is a downer; forgiveness is uplifting. I have learned to choose to get past my anger and to be the first to offer an olive branch, even to people I dislike, because it makes me feel better.

Hanging on to anger with people was not good for either of us. This happened to me much too often, as I had a quick temper, impatience with people, and a strong sense of when I was wronged. I used to hang onto these feelings, which certainly interfered with my overall happiness.

I discovered that once I got past adolescence, I always felt better by giving a loved one a well-thought-out gift, rather than by receiving one that I really wanted. It is a long road from selfishness to selflessness.

Self-esteem promotes happiness. I learned that if I strove to be the best at any endeavor (except golf), giving it my best effort, and achieving it, brought both self-esteem and happiness. If I fell short, I determined to try again. Happy people accomplish more.

Happiness is truly a choice. We can choose to be optimistic, setting expectations just high enough. We can look at life's setbacks and brood over them, or we can look at the bright side of things. When I lost my job as general manager of Intermetrics' Aerospace Systems Group and was out of work for five months during a major recession in the industry, it would have been easy to get down on the environment and myself, but I refused. By working every day to find a new, fulfilling job in my field, I remained optimistic and upbeat, making myself stronger through small successes.

Here are some ways to be happy, according to Jeff Nader of *Entrepreneur Magazine Inc*:

Sleep More: You will be less sensitive to negative emotions

Spend More Time with Friends and Family

Get Outdoors More

Help Others 100 Hours per Year

Exercise: Even a short time will help

Practice Smiling and Mean it

Plan a Trip, even if you don't go

Move Closer to Work: A short commute is worth more than a big house

Practice Gratitude

Stay away from grouchy people

Keep learning

Laugh Often, Long, and Loud

Do Not Take Guilt Trips

Tell People You Love That You Love Them

BIBLIOGRAPHY

Boles, Richard N. (1970). What Color is Your Parachute? New York, NY, Random House

Carlson, Richard (2005), Easier Than You Think: Because Life Doesn't Have to be So Hard, New York, NY, HarperCollins

Gray, John (1992), Men Are from Mars, Women Are from Venus, New York, NY, HarperCollins

Haft, Alan (2008), You Can Never Be Too Rich, Hoboken, NJ, John Wiley & Sons

Lucht, John (1988), Rites of Passage at $100,000+, New York, NY, The Viceroy Press

Peale, Norman Vincent (1952), The Power of Positive Thinking, Upper Saddle River, NJ, Prentice Hall

Peck, M. Scott (1999), Golf and the Spirit, New York, NY, Three Rivers Press

Ross, Hugh N. (1998), The Genesis Question: Scientific Advances and the Accuracy of Genesis, Colorado Springs, CO, Nav Press

Schweizer, Peter (2020), Profiles in Corruption: Abuse of Power by America's Progressive Elite, New York, NY, HarperCollins

Strobel, Lee P. (1998), The Case for Christ, Grand Rapids, Michigan, Zondervan

Town, Phillip B. (2010), Payback Time: Making Big Money is the Best Revenge, New York, NY, Random House

ACKNOWLEDGEMENTS

A big debt of gratitude to my wife, Sue, who greatly improved the style and content of this book. She also censored content that was too personal and otherwise might have embarrassed someone, including me.

I offer another thank you to my granddaughter, Taylor Odish, for once again creating an interesting cover using her skills as a graphic designer.

I especially thank Peggy Williams for her eagle eye in discovering errors that escaped my diligent proof-reading exercises. She has a special talent.

ABOUT THE AUTHOR

Kurth Krause was born in Milwaukee in 1940. He received his Bachelor of Science degree in mathematics and physics from the University of Wisconsin in 1962. He studied astronautical guidance in graduate school at the Massachusetts Institute of Technology in 1965. Kurth received management training at the UCLA Graduate School of Management and the Stanford Executive Institute. He has been married to Susan (Firle) Krause since 1963. They reside in Rancho Mission Viejo, California. They have two children and four grandchildren.

Kurth became a pioneer in the space field; at age 25, while at MIT he wrote vital subroutines of the guidance and navigation software for the Apollo Command Module and Lunar Module flight computers which flew in every Apollo mission. He and Sue witnessed the launch of Apollo 11 from the astronaut viewing area at Cape Canaveral. At age 28, Kurth sat at the guidance console in the Houston backup Mission Control Room while Neil Armstrong and Buzz Aldrin landed on the moon.

Kurth's first book, *My 36 Years in Space*, was first published in 2016, and a second edition in 2019. It received five stars from all Amazon reviewers and a top rating from the Online Book Club:

Official Review:

My 36 Years in Space by Kurth Krause

10 ... 9 ... 8 ... Engine Ignition! 7 ...6 ... 5... 4 ... 3 ... 2 ... We have liftoff!

This countdown would launch Apollo 11 toward a mission the media called "the greatest accomplishment of the decade." On July 20, 1969, man first stepped on the Moon, a historical event watched around the world. Through the lens of Kurth Krause's space engineering career, readers come to know how events unfolded during one of the most dangerous space missions ever attempted, as highlighted in *My 36 Years in Space: An Astronautical Engineer's Journey through the Triumphs and Tragedies of America's Space Programs*. A team of masterminds managed to land two astronauts on the Moon's surface. But would they be able to bring them back safely?

Launching a rocket into space is a complex process, but it is not as complicated as guiding it back to Earth from another celestial body in our solar system, such as the Moon. As a young engineer, Kurth Krause is tasked to develop an onboard program to be used on the Command Module (CM) and the Lunar Module (LM) to facilitate a return-to-earth mission during the Apollo Era. It all begins in a rather technologically primitive period when computer science, missile engineering curricula, and space science were still limited. Krause highlights some of the challenges and space achievements that America went through at a time when the space race was a determinant for global dominance and supremacy. In addition, the writer gives a glimpse into his personal family life and how he balanced this with his highly demanding work.

This book was an exhilarating read for me, making me aware of rather mind-blowing scientific principles. The absorbing storytelling kept me completely engaged. With my minimal knowledge of astronomy and space programs, I was excited to better understand the astronautical wisdom that the author poured into his work, complements of a thirty-six-year career in the space field. Reading about the intellectual accomplishments of these men was truly awe-inspiring. Delving into this non-fiction piece may seem intimidating, even burdensome. The text contains scientific terms that were a bit complicated but not incomprehensible.

If you are not a "rocket science" geek but wish to better understand the space world, this book provides a thrilling and comprehensible journey through America's space programs. I managed to navigate the complexity of this work with little difficulty. Somehow it became easier to understand, and in the end, a feeling of absolute marvel took over me. It was impressive.

Krause thoroughly describes the difficult mission and the amazing triumph of Armstrong, Buzz Aldrin, and the entire space crew. I imagined how glorious this event must have been — especially viewing it live in 1969. I thought of Neil Armstrong's first words while stepping down on lunar soil: "One small step for a man, one giant leap for mankind."

The author self-describes in the book as someone whose "doodling included playing with Fibonacci numbers, infinite series, singularities, and deriving trig identities." Anyone who relates to that will definitely enjoy the book. But you don't need a background in math or science to find the work compelling and understandable. It can also be recommended to students who aspire to a career in space program engineering; it will give you a closer look at the Apollo Space Program, NASA customers, and aerospace career.

    I encountered no grammatical errors, and the well-edited book allowed for easy reading. The absence of expletives was no surprise for a book of this class. The author also made good use of pictures, which made it easier for me to grasp the scientific concepts being described. *My 36 Years in Space*, by Kurth Krause, deeply deserves a 4 out of 4 stars rating to the moon and back.

www.ingramcontent.com/pod-product-compliance
Lightning Source LLC
Chambersburg PA
CBHW070601010526
44118CB00012B/1406